The Spirits, Secrets and Sins of the City by The Sea

A behind the scenes peek at the outlandish, bizarre, unexplained, yet true tales of Newport, Rhode Island.

Contents

INTRODUCTION 3
1 PIRATES PAY THE PRICE 10
2 MYSTERY AT AMERICA"S OLDEST TAVERN 19
3 AMERICA'S MOST HAUNTED STREET? 26
4 A SECRET STACKED IN STONE 40
5 AMERICA'S ROYAL FAMILY 49
6 LEAP OF FAITH 63
7 CONSPIRACIES ON THE HIGH SEAS 70
8 U.S.S. BENNINGTON 79
9 THE RESTLESS SPIRIT OF ROSE ISLAND 88
10 THE HOUSE ON A ROCK 94
11 HURRICANE HUT 105
12 CHAOS AT CROSSWAYS 111
13 THE POOR LITTLE RICH GIRL 121
14 REVERSAL OF FORTUNE 140
15 TITANIC DECISIONS 151
16 ALVA 164
17 MRS. MAKE-A-LISTER 180
18 THE MANSION ON THE MOVE 188
19 CURSED FORTUNE? 195
20 THE MOST ROBBED WOMAN IN AMERICA 215
21 IN YOUR FACE MRS. ASTOR 220
22 GET DOWN OFF YOUR HIGH HORSE 227
23 DARKNESS ON THE EDGE OF TOWN 235

Introduction

Since its founding in 1639, Newport, Rhode Island has been no stranger to controversy. Founded as a haven for religious freedom seekers, Newport has evolved and morphed numerous times to reflect the economic and social climate of the times. Thanks to its geography along with its deep and well protected harbor, the City by the Sea, flourished as a haven for pirates, ship captains, traders, merchants, craftsmen and seafarers all before the American Revolution. Giving Newport a profitable yet controversial role in the potentiality lucrative triangle trade.

Newport's location, situated neatly between Boston to the North and New York City to the southwest, made it a prime target for the British to invade, overtake and encamp for 3 years beginning in December of 1776. From this strategic location, The British strategy was to launch attacks to overtake Boston, but the plans never came to fruition, and when the British ultimately departed in 1779, the once busting seaport town was left a smoldering wreck, never to regain its prominence as a commercial center. These actions from 4 centuries ago, still resonate in the local economy today.

After the British departure, the French arrived as allies and assisted the Continental Army defeat the British at the Battle of Yorktown in Virginia, securing our (The

United States' Independence) French commander Rochambeau even met with General George Washington in Newport, at the Vernon House on Clarke Street, once again demonstrating Newport's significance as a key cog in the role of obtaining Independence.

Once the American Revolution subsided, Newport had become somewhat of an afterthought, subsiding on fishing to eke out a living. Factories were being built further North along the rivers near Providence, the triangle trade had been outlawed and Newport descended into an economic depression that would last 5 decades. Ironically, the tides of change would arrive, and the economic clouds would dissipate, albeit from an unlikely source, Southern Plantation Owners.

The year is 1839, and a plantation owner named George Noble Jones irrevocably changes this seaside town's fortunes forever. Mr. Jones is very wealthy, as the proprietor of "Wormsloe" plantation just outside of Savannah, Georgia and the 8000-acre cotton plantation, 'El Destino" in North Central Florida, not far from the present-day Capital of Florida, Tallahassee. However, one thing all the money in the world couldn't buy at that time was air conditioning, which of course had not been invented yet. As you could imagine, summers in the South in the 19th century would be excruciatingly hot and humid. So, Mr. Jones went North for the summer to enjoy his time, built a summer cottage called Kingscote, starting a building boom along previously undeveloped Bellevue Avenue.

Once again, the winds of war would alter Newport fortunes, of course from a distance this time, with the

Civil War raging throughout the Nation. The southern plantation owners and their Antebellum Cottages would be replaced, post war, by previously unimaginable wealth, created from the Industrial Revolution, New York City Real Estate booms and mining. Many of the southern plantation owners would never return to Newport after the civil war, with their fortunes gone and their plantations in ruins from the conflict. A new generation of wealth was ready to step in, with their massive bankrolls and talented architects, they would replicate European Palaces, along Bellevue Avenue and eventually Ocean Drive, with each family trying to outdo the other, culminating in the crown jewel of all Newport estates, The Breakers.

The building boom continued through the turn of the next century and the "Who's Who" from the wealthiest and most influential families spent their summer months out of the large east coast cities and along the cool coastline of the Ocean State. The Mrs. Astor of New York City even created her own social registry known as the "400" where the old money Knickerbockers would be included, just because of their family lineage. The list was so exclusive that the Nouveau Riche like the Vanderbilts, and their railroad fortune or Edward Berwin, whose money came from a dirty business, coal mining, would be excluded. Mrs. Astor's social influence would earn Newport the title as "The Queen of Summer Resorts."

The good times would roll on, the champagne flowed all summer long and the summer crowds would continue to flood to the area beaches until a stock market crash and the great depression ensued, once again altering

Newport's trajectory as a summer seaside resort town. Many of the Bellevue Avenue mansions would be abandoned, torn down, or repurposed for other uses during the 1930's and early 1940's.

By 1941 and the United States inclusion into World War II, almost the entire Newport region was transformed into a miliary instillation. Once again, the geography played a role in Newport's wartime footing and transformation. Newport would be transformed into one of the largest naval stations in the U.S. with an Air Station across Narragansett Bay, a P.T Boat training facility in Portsmouth and the largest torpedo factory in the world, on Goat Island. Newport and the surrounding area played their part in winning the war.

Even after the war, Newport would be considered a "Navy Town" where young sailors did their training, over 100 ships called Naval Station Newport their home port, and the Naval War college educated the top brass of the Maritime Branch of the armed forces.

But of course, this would all change again, with the Presidential election of 1972. President Richard Nixon, in a vindictive manner, wanted to punish the only region of the United States, who did not support his re-election bid against George McGovern. So, with the stroke of a pen, Nixon closed the Boston Navy Shipyard and Naval Station Newport in 1974 as a political vendetta. The cruiser- destroyer fleet was re-deployed to Norfolk, Virginia, an area which Nixon had carried heavily in his re-election bid, and with the re-deployment of the fleet went 1000's of navy families, 15,000 civilian jobs and Newport's main driver of the local economy. Once again, the region would have to re-invent itself and fast.

What would a town, so dependent on military spending do, to quickly re-position itself to avoid another prolonged economic disaster? Newport would go back to its hospitality and tourism roots and roll out the red carpet to visitors, to celebrate the nations bicentennial in 1976.

The Newport, Pell Bridge had recently been completed and a feeder road, to deliver cars to the waterfront, known as America's Cup Avenue, was hastily completed. But to get these arriving visitors a sacrifice had to be made. To complete its route, it had to be constructed, by literally sawing a historic neighborhood, known as the Point, in half. But all in the name of progress and keeping the economic engine moving forward. To celebrate the bicentennial and usher Newport into its new phase of life, a Tall Ships Event was scheduled and was a monstrous success. 10's of thousands of visitors arrived, swarming the newly gentrified Downtown Waterfront, and announcing to the World, Newport, Rhode Island was open for tourism. Most of the historic downtown Waterfront was quickly scrubbed clean of all traces of a once bustling and somewhat nefarious "Navy Town." So, the tattoo parlors, pawn shops and burlesque halls were irrevocably transformed into tony fine dining restaurants, high end shopping wharfs and luxury waterfront hotels. As a matter of fact, when many Navy Vets come back for a ship's reunion, they almost always, without question will say, "I don't recognize the place."

Will Newport need to evolve again? It is hard to say or know what the future holds. One thing is for sure, it is unlikely the area will need to transform anytime soon, cementing itself as one of the premier summer destinations along the East Coast of the United States. A quick walk along the downtown waterfront will give you an indication that Newport has regained its status from the late 1800's as the "Queen of Summer Resorts." When you take a look at the size of the yachts, sailboats and the price of real estate along Bellevue Avenue, there is no question Newport is once again at the top of the list for this country and the world's wealthy and elite, to idle away their summers. And the good news for us, there is plenty for the rest of the 99.9 percenters to do and explore here in the "City by the Sea."

There is one thing however, the rest of the 99.9 percenters need from the super wealthy, however. We need their propensity to cause some scandalous event, try to keep it a secret with a coverup, or create a ghost, trying to make their scandalous catastrophe disappear. Thankfully, for the sake of this book, they aren't very good at it, leaving us plenty of Spirits, Secrets and Sins to share with you, from more than 380+ years of Newport history.

So now, we have a brief historical background as how we arrived at the current day place, we all enjoy. But let's get to the good stuff and peel back the curtain and discover how all those Sprits, Secrets and Sins evolved!

We have added some references for the fans of the HBO series the Gilded Age, much of which was filmed in Newport, Rhode Island.

We included a few filming locations as well where the real-life characters from the show spent their summer seasons. We find the series an invaluable peek into how these wealthy families spent their summers and fortunes, trying to leave indelible marks on history with their extravagant Mansion Building. (All for a 6-to-8-week summer get away!)

Copyright 2024 All Rights Reserved

Front and back cover images were property of the author or acquired in the public domain.

1

Pirates pay the Price

Piracy was a profitable and somewhat acceptable profession for some of the 17th and early 18th century along the east coast of the British colonies all the way south through the Caribbean Islands, along the Northern, South American coast. Even the west coast of Africa was known for pirate raids, extending into the early 19th century. Keep in mind even the Marine Anthem mentions the conflict known at the Barbary Wars:

From the Halls of Montezuma

To the shores of Tripoli (North Africa and the Barbary Coast.)

We fight our country's battles

In the air, on land, and sea....

Essentially piracy, in its simplest form was the raiding of others ships for their cargo, impressing or killing the overtaken crew and either selling or consuming the ill begotten goods pilfered from the overrun sailing vessel. Rhode Island was well known throughout the

Colonies for its piracy, with local marauder, Thomas Tew being the most infamous. The colony was un affectionately called "Rogues Island", during this time as well. During this period known as the "Golden Age of Piracy" raiders took up an almost legendary status, with their fearsome looks, blood thirsty crews and foreboding pirate flags, which would send shivers through opposing crews, even before a seaborne battle had occurred. One way to say it would be, their violent and unforgiving reputation preceded them.

Even to this day, we still know the names of some of these legendary pirates, forever remembered in the lore of the high seas. Famous pirates from this period included "Black Sam" Bellamy, Henry Morgan, William "Captain" Kidd, "Calico" Jack Rackham, Bartholomew Roberts and the terrifying Blackbeard, whose real name was Edward Teach. Even the ladies got involved in the plundering, with Anny Bonney and Mary Read still well known to Pirate aficionados. Let's be perfectly clear, these were not upstanding citizens to be emulated. They were essential murderers and criminals. Edward Low was infamous for torturing opposing captains in particularly heinous ways before ultimately ending their lives. Finally, the British crown had enough, the high seas piracy was not only cutting into their customs collection and revenue, but the terror on the seas was also negatively affecting their citizens and Royal Navy sailors, who if captured would be forced in plundering for their captors or face death.

The European governments were really starting to feel the strain and would enact laws to curb piracy, while their Navies would ramp up their patrols to turn the hunters into the hunted. On September 5, 1717, King George I issued the "Proclamation for Suppressing of Pirates": The King's Pardon. The British Crown was willing to grant clemency to any pirate who surrendered themselves to a governor of the colonies by September 5, 1718. Hundreds of pirates who believed they would be criminals and fugitives until they died were suddenly free to return to society. The offer was simply too good for many to pass up, wiping the slate clean, and allowing them essentially a free pass and forgive all previous sins! Another important factor in the ending of the pirate era, was the appointment of a British Captain Woodes Rogers as Governor in Chief of Nassau in the Bahamas. Let's just say, things were about to change in "Mr. Roger's" neighborhood. Nassau, once known as the safest of safe havens for harboring pirates, would do a complete 180. Forts guarding the harbor were reinforced, the British Navy presence was increased and even former pirates, like the notorious Benjamin Hardigold, switched sides and became a pirate hunter for the crown.

Piracy would still continue, albeit with fewer ships and marauders involved into the early 1720's. On June 10th,1723, a British 20 gunned man of war, H.M.S. Greyhound, had been sailing along the east coast, and encountered 2 pirate sloops, The Ranger, and The Fortune, captained by perhaps the most violent pirate of the day, Edward Low. The pirate sloops, made a colossal error, thinking the heavily gunned war ship was actually a merchant vessel, and attacked under their Black Flag. Once the pirate fleet engaged the Greyhound in battle, they quickly realized they were outgunned, and had made a huge miscalculation, but it was too late. The British warship prevailed and was able to capture the Ranger and tow it to Newport, for the crew to stand trial. Edward Low was able to escape on a smaller vessel, with a skeleton crew, fleeing across the Atlantic to the Azores. But his increased raids and violent attacks made him priority #1 for the British Admiralty and his freedom would be fleeting. A trial was held in

Newport and the verdict was swift, 26 members of the crew were sentenced to death by hanging. The day of reckoning finally arrived, July 19th, 1723, at a location many of you have probably strolled past, never realizing what had occurred there that fateful day. It is called Gravelly point, located on the west end of Long Wharf, just past the Newport Yacht Club. Of course, in those days, it was just a long, somewhat jagged wharf extending close to 1000 feet, from the west side of Thames Street, crossing over the tidal marsh known as the "Basin" and reaching a sand and gravel sliver of land, where ultimately 26 doomed souls would meet their end. We are talking almost 300 years before the Marriott, Wyndham Long Wharf time share Resort, the Newport Lobster Shack, and the Marriott Hotel, to name a few modern landmarks, ever existed. You won't find Gravelly Point on any modern tourist maps, because essentially it doesn't exist anymore. A timeshare property has been built on top of it. A time share resort literally sits on top of a location where 26 doomed men met their fate for acts of Piracy in 1723. How is that for progress?

26 Pirates met a similar fate at Gravelly Point, just off Long Wharf, in Downtown Newport, RI.

The method for the execution, short drop hanging, was particularly cruel and painful, but fit the crimes of the convicted, Piracy, robbery, and larceny. A large jubilant crown had gathered to witness the event, still the largest public execution in the history of the America's, and quickly realized the method chosen was particularly painful and prolonged. Short drop hanging is more like a slow choking method of torture, taking victims between 5 and 45 minutes to ultimately perish. Witness' reported some men turned a purplish-blue color, while others had muffled screams from their tongues protruding and even eyeballs bulging out of their sockets from the ropes pressure. There was no ambiguity with these public executions, Newport, Rhode Island was off limits to pirates, period. Local officials wanted to make it clear, with no gray area that Pirates would be put to death. And like a warning flag along Newport Harbor and Narragansetts bay, the lifeless bodies would hang for more than 3 months at this prominent location, with their pirate flag, flying on the gallows with them. One can hardly imagine a starker warning, that the "Golden Age of Piracy" had come to a violent end! News of the doomed men spread quicky. Even legendary preacher Cotton Mather of Boston warned his parishioners of the fate that awaited anyone involved in this perilous trade after word spread of the executions 70 miles to the south.

"If you will not hear the warnings of your faithful pastors, hear the roarings of twenty-six terrible preachers that, in a ghastly apparition are now from the dead, calling you to turn and live unto God."

It wasn't until late October 1723, when the hanging hoods were removed, the decomposing bodies were cut down, and the remains were shipped across the bay to Goat Island. You may know Goat Island today as home to a luxury hotel, a marina with multimillion-dollar yachts and high-end condos. But the Island was chosen for a specific reason, one much more sinister, not as scenic location for 26 doomed souls to finally rest in peace. Almost as a final way to inflict an eternity of unrest, the southern tip of the tiny Island was chosen, and the ill-fated souls were buried at the exact mid-point between the high and low tide. This location would ensure that for all time, the waters of Narragansett Bay would wash over their buried corpse for all eternity.

What became of the most violent and torturous pirate of his day, Edward Low? It actually depends on which story you believe. There were rumors, Low was sailing for Brazil from Africa and his ship sank on the voyage in a violent storm. The mostly likely outcome was Low was set adrift without provisions from his captured ship "Merry Christmas" when the crew mutinied after Captain Low had violently killed a crew member in his sleep. Apparently even other pirates grew weary of Low's violent, unpredictable, and murderous outbursts. Edward Low would actually be rescued by a passing French ship. However, his jubilance from rescue in the Middle of the Caribbean Sea would be short lived. The French authorities would discover the identity of the adrift sailor, and Edward Low was hanged in Martinique in 1724.

With Low's death, either from a violent storm or hanging and the 26 pirate publicly executed at Gravelly Point, Piracy, for all intents and purposed died with them. This final chapter of the "Golden Age of Piracy" book was written with violent and emphatic results and would close the manuscript forever, at least in this part of the world.

2

Mystery at America's Oldest Tavern

Imagine you sailed into Newport, in the early 1700's, and needed a place to grab a bite to eat and a place to sleep with a solid roof over your head, before re-boarding your ship, for another long voyage at sea. Newport had such a place dubbed "America's Oldest Tavern" so you would be in luck. Now keep in mind almost every colonial city and town has what they claim is "America's Oldest Tavern." The White Horse Tavern, still located on the corner of West Marlborough and Farewell Streets, has the resume to make that claim. The tavern's location is well situated for arriving sailors to walk a handful of blocks from the Wharf area and find a place to stay.

The tavern dates back to 1652 when a man named Francis Brinley built a small structure on the corner of Marlborough and Farewell Streets, then sold the property to William Mayes Sr. in 1673 and enlarged the structure to its present dimensions. In 1702 with William Jr. as proprietor, perhaps with his local political connections, was able to attain a tavern license which would legally allow the White Horse "to sell all sorts of strong drink." You see William Jr. had an interesting side hustle. He was a legal pirate, known as a privateer. Both were basically pirates, raiding commercial vessels on the high seas, and pillaging the cargo discovered on the overtaken ship. However, the one huge difference was a privateer basically had a license to steal, they held in their possession a charter from a colonial governor, making it permissible to take whatever they encountered on their voyages. There was one big caveat, in exchange for the privateer charter, the stolen cargo had to be divided and given to the Colonial Governor who issued the decree, basically a kick-back for granting the pact. William Mayes Jr. was very successful on his voyages, especially on the Red Sea. As far as we can tell though, Mayes Jr. is not the ghost wandering the 17th century structure. The spirit that lingers on the 2nd floor of the tavern may have come from a cryptic incident, that occurred in the early 1730's.

2 men would arrive and request a room from the current innkeeper, Mary Mayes Nichols, who has taken over operations from her notorious privateering brother, William Jr. There was nothing uncommon about such a request, The White Horse Tavern was a popular place for a simple and inexpensive place to spend the night. In some ports-of-call, overnight sleeping arrangements weren't always easy to find. Some seaport towns didn't openly welcome strange Ocean bound guests, who weren't always the most refined of visitors and were reputed to drink, fight and generally cause problems once they arrived on land. In some coastal colonial towns, the best you could find would be a barn filled with hay or a stable to be shared with horses. Newport was much different, with varying degrees of lodging establishments dotting the waterfront. And by all accounts these 2 men were nothing out of the ordinary. They had a small meal on the lower level of the tavern, then retired to the 2nd floor, unfurled a small mat on the floor and went to sleep in front of the ample fireplace. Nothing raised Mary's alarms about these 2 visitors, everything seemed fine, until the next morning arrived.

Mary and her Native American assistant awoke early the next day, to prepare some breakfast for their overnight guests, but something was amiss. The 2 mystery sailors never come down to eat. So, the pair of ladies proceeded up the narrow staircase to the upstairs room and were shocked at what they discovered! One of the unknown travelers lay dead on the floor, in front of the large stone fireplace where he slept. The 2nd man was gone, vanished in the night without a trace, with the dead man's belongings in tow. Yet there was no sign of a struggle, no visible wounds could be seen, nor a drop of blood was found. To make matters worse, smallpox was a public health concern and since both women had come in contact with the deceased traveler, Mary Mayes Nichols and her native American assistant were quickly whisked off to quarantine on nearby Coaster's Island, the current site of the Naval War College, just north of the Newport, Pell Bridge. The unnamed visitor's body was hastily disposed of in a pauper's grave, quickly dug in Newport's Common Burying ground, in hopes to stall the spread of deadly smallpox.

The worse fears would come to pass, both Mary and her assistant contracted the highly contagious disease, with Mary eventually overcoming her illness, but the native American assistant was not so fortunate. She would succumb to the deadly virus a short time later.

And what became of the mystery traveler, who disappeared in the middle of the night? That saga is still unsolved to this day. There is a small clue however that the man who died on the 2nd floor, did not perish of natural causes. As ghost hunters and paranormal investigators will tell us, a ghost will often return from beyond the grave, to seek revenge on the person who may have ended their life, prematurely. There have been no shortage of ghost stories, unexplained sightings, and footsteps throughout the upper level of the White Horse Tavern. Most sighting mysteriously occur, directly in front of the fireplace, where the mystery traveler was found dead. Is that a coincidence or a solid indication of what actually occurred that fateful night? Employees over the years at the White Horse Tavern, have a similar tale. They hear footsteps on the 2nd floor constantly around closing time, as if someone was anxiously pacing the floor above. Waitstaff has even grabbed a peppermill as a weapon and gone up the staircase to investigate, expecting to encounter an intruder, yet no human is ever there. Another popular story, especially amongst the bartenders, is they have frequently sighted a slightly built man, with long hair and dressed like he stepped off a Clipper ship from the 18th century. The reports of the spectral visitor from a by gone era, is always seen in the same location, directly in front of the stone fireplace, where the lifeless body of the mystery traveler was found that fateful morning. If these reports are accurate, then we have a clue to what actually occurred that evening, more than 3 centuries ago. The unlucky victim was most likely murdered, perhaps asphyxiated as he slept, while his bunkmate stole his earthly belongings, slipped quietly out of the Tavern and into the night. The revenge seeking apparition is likely hanging around where his life was snuffed out, hoping to one day exact revenge on his killer. Apparently, ghosts are very patient, and his presence will likely haunt this location for all eternity.

So, if you are in Newport, and want to step back in time and enjoy a fine dining experience, The White Horse Tavern is an excellent choice. Or grab their signature cocktail, a dark and stormy, and sit by the bar and see if the vengeful spirit makes an appearance. Don't worry if you spot him, he isn't out to get you, unless of course you were the murderer…

The Historic and Haunted White Horse Tavern has stood on the corners of West Marlborough and Farewell Street since 1639.

(Photo courtesy of the author.)

3

America's Most Haunted Street?

Thanks to our friends, at Ghost Tours of Newport, RI. for pointing this out to us, but the most haunted street in the U. S. of A. might be right here in the City by the Sea. Starting on the corner of Touro and Clarke Streets, with the vaudeville era Jane Pickens theatre and ending at the Vernon House, just a short 3 blocks away, there are at least 5 locations with paranormal activity.

Clarke Street is named for one of the 9 original British settlers of Newport, Dr. John Clarke, a Baptist minister, founder of the United Baptist Church and local philanthropist. Dr. Clarke also donated the roughly 10 acres of land to the city where the Common Burying grounds sits today.

So how could a street so short, earn the moniker, "The most haunted street in America?" It really comes down to the historical buildings that have survived almost 3 centuries as well as some of the occupants over the years of these historic structures.

Keep in mind, we are going to detail each structure and the possible origin of each apparition currently haunting each structure from north to south. Clarke Street is a one-way thoroughfare! The Jane Pickens Theater, named for a prominent Broadway actress of the 1940's and 50, prominently occupies the corner. With its large movie marque, it is hard to miss. First built as the Zion Episcopal Church in 1834, then St Joseph's Catholic Church in 1885, then a live theater for just a few years in 1910's and finally found its niche in 1922 when it became a movie palace known as The Strand with the advent of silent film. Apparently, the resident spirit who haunts the balcony harkens back to her days her enjoying these silent movies. According to Ghost Tours of Newport, who have been leading evening Ghost Walks throughout Newport's colonial district for more than 20 years, this location wasn't an original stop on their popular tour. One evening a frantic projectionist stopped the guide mid-tour and was so compelled about what he witnessed, Ghost Tours of Newport was intrigued and had to investigate for themselves. The theatre projectionist said he had a bizarre dream that a spirit was trapped behind the wall in the projection booth and wanted to escape their entrapment from behind their entombment. The employee also said he felt a cold presence on his right shoulder, that seemed to follow him as he ascended and descended the small ladder which led to his perch high above the theatre's patrons. Based on these firsthand accounts, Ghost Tours of Newport. RI. called on their resident psychic and headed inside to investigate the repoerted paranormal activity. After proceeding to the balcony area directly below the ladder to the projection booth, the psychic made contact! And, wow, the spirit had a lot to say. According to the intermediary, the spirit identified herself as Gladys Mumford, and had attended the movie theatre as a young girl, particularly enjoying the silent films once shown on the silver screen. She reminisced about those silent screen stars from that by-gone era like Greta Garbo, Rudolph Valentino and "America's Sweetheart" Mary Pickford. When Gladys passed away in the 1960's her spirit returned to the one place, she was truly happy during her life.

Just a half a block further down Clarke Street, there is an impressive 2 story stone building with a double wooden door, with an abundance of paranormal activity inside. The sturdy stone structure, known as the Newport Artillery Company, has quite an impressive historical resume. The Artillery company is the oldest chartered military company remaining in the United States, established in 1741 from a decree from King George II of England. The current building onsite was completed in 1835 and the second floor was added after a devastating fire in 1906. The property now functions as a military museum and currently houses over 50 vintage military uniforms from all over the world. The pride of their collection is 4 bronze canons forged in Boston by Silversmith Paul Revere in 1798... Yes, that Paul Revere! And despite the age of the vintage canons, the Artillery Company still fires them on a ceremonial basic, especially to celebrate the 4th of July.

The ghostly activity is mostly concentrated on the second level, according to the members of the Artillery Company themselves. Many evenings, the members of the Artillery Company will spend a late night preparing their canons for a parade or ceremony the following day. That's when the footsteps begin, as if an invisible squadron of soldiers are marching in unison above. Members have also reported hearing drumbeats and even the sound of a bugle as if an infantryman is signaling out his fellow ghost soldiers to line up in formation. There is no doubt, spirits with a military past still roam this historic and heroic structure.

The popular Ghost Tours of Newport, showing their guests the Artillery Company building, along what could be considered, "The most haunted street in America!"

(Photo courtesy of Ghost Tours of Newport, RI.)

Almost directly across the street, on the opposite side from the artillery company, is an impressive green, 3 story Georgian Colonial, which is currently called the Clarkeston Inn. The property built in 1705 is now part of the Inns of Newport collection owned by a local innkeeper named Rick. Over his years of ownership, Rick has heard numerous bizarre and hair-raising stories from his time as Innkeeper, but there is one tale that constantly emanated from the 3rd floor of the venerable Clarkeston Inn. Guests will mention that the lights will mysteriously turn on, especially in the middle of the night. There is a clue to perhaps the ghost might be wandering the 3rd floor of the haunted inn. America's first lighthouse keeper, Ida Lewis once lived in the inn when it was a private home. She labored at the nearby at the Lime Rock Lighthouse, guarding the entrance to Newport Harbor, for more than 50 years… She was credited with saving 18 lives as a lighthouse keeper. She was awarded a gold medal for her lifesaving efforts, was the highest paid keeper of her day ($750 a year!), and was so famous, President Ulysses S. Grant, asked to meet her during his visit. So perhaps as a lifelong lighthouse keeper she had one mission, that has carried on into the afterlife, the motto of every lighthouse keeper: THE LIGHT MUST STAY ON!

Across the street from the Clarkeston Inn is another colonial property also part of the Inns of Newport collection, The Admiral Farragut Inn. A former owner of the Inn reportedly had a pet cat that refused to go into room 4 on the 2nd floor. The cat would screech anytime it came close to this room, with the hair standing up on the back of its neck. There were also times the cat would stare into the empty room, with its eyes moving side to side, as if it was watching someone or something move around the room. Even though humas eyes would see not a living soul insight! As it turns out, the home was occupied by the French Army, our allies during the American revolution. High ranking French officers quartered in the high-end property in 1780. Multiple guests and staff have repeatedly seen an apparition, nattily dressed in an 18th century French military uniform, descending rapidly from the back of the property and into the basement. 2 very high-ranking aide-de-camp, lodged here during the almost 1-year French occupation, Axel de Ferson and the Marquis de Damas. Evidently, the one of French officers enjoyed his time here, and returned to Clarke Street after his death. As you can see there is a lot of paranormal activity on this very short street. And we still need to tell you about the most active paranormal site, located at the end of the street, The Vernon House.

The very impressive 2 and ½ story wooden structure, with twin chimneys and 3 dormers, was enlarged in 1759 by a justice of the colonial supreme court named Metcalf Bowler. Judge Bowler wanted to display his wealth and prominence by doubling the size of the original structure and hired a noted colonial architect named Peter Harrison to carry out the extensive project. If you have the good fortune to see the impressive home in person, you will swear it's made of blocks of stone. However, that was a signature design of the architect, who also designed other prominent Newport Landmarks like the Touro Synagogue and the Redwood Library. Harrison was famous for using a technique called rustication, where blocks of wood would be cut and treated with sand, giving the illusion that the wooden structure was actually constructed of stone. George Washington was so impressed with the handsome exterior he replicated the look on his home, Mount Vernon in Virginia, but we'll get to his visit a bit later.

The home was eventually sold to a powerful local merchant who was heavily involved in the shameful and vile Triangle Trade, William Vernon in 1773. Vernon's timing to purchase the home wasn't ideal however, the British army overtook Newport in December 1776. Many local merchants who were pro-revolution like William Vernon, fled the town, for Massachusetts, while the British Army occupied the city for 3 long years. The British occupation was the death knell for the once prominent seaport. It was observed that the 3 winters the British spend in Newport were historically cold and frigid. After literally chopping down every tree on Aquidneck Island for firewood, the vengeful British in an attempt not to freeze to death, started ripping apart Colonial Homes, board by board, for firewood. Although no official count was ever kept, reports say more than 200 colonial structures were damaged or destroyed during the occupation. Thankfully, the stately Vernon House survived this dark time in Newport.

The British troops finally departed Newport, in late 1779 to lay siege to the largest coastal southern port at the time, Charleston, South Carolina. On their way out of port, the ruthless Brits, as one final farewell, burned the

Jamestown Lighthouse to the ground, not before stealing the lens on their voyage southward.

In July of 1780, a ray of light finally shone, and the dark clouds parted on the decimated City by the Sea, with a flotilla of French ships and a garrison of French troops numbering nearly 6000 arriving on the shore under the command of Marshal Jean-Baptiste Donatien de Vimeur, comte de Rochambeau. A very impressive title to say the least, but going forward, we shall refer to him as General Rochambeau! The general was no doubt, a man of refined taste, chose the regal Vernon House as his headquarters. In March 1781, General Rochambeau hosted General George Washington, where they discussed battle plans on how to defeat the British. The plan to vanquish their mutual foe would come to fruition in October of 1781, with a victory at Yorktown, Virginia. The combined land forces blocked a retreat on 1 side of the narrow peninsula, with the French Fleet blockading the other, preventing a water escape route. British General Lord Cornwallis had no other option but to lay down his sword, and agree to the terms of surrender, ensuring Independence for the Colonies and the founding of the United States of America.

As much as we wish we could claim the poltergeist that currently haunts the Vernon House, was the spirit of one this nation's greatest Ally's, General Rochambeau, the evidence points to a previous owner with a sinister double life. Most of the evidence points toward former owner, Judge Metcalf Bowler, who as it turns out was actually a double agent and spy for the British. During the 1920's, a researcher cataloging of the papers of General Sir Henry Clinton, commander of the occupying British Army in Newport, discovered correspondence revealing Judge Bowler was a paid informant. All this time Bowler was still a Rhode Island Supreme Court Justice, and open critic of British oppression and occupation. Through these extensive letters it seems like Judge Bowler was attempting to curry favor with the oppressing Powers to be to save his vast real estate holding from being seized.

The most credible ghost sightings from the Vernon House came from longtime owner, Margareta Culow, who had more than one run in with the restless and seemingly disgruntled spirit. One evening Margareta was hosting an intimate dinner party and noticed a tall, slender figure dressed as if he stepped out of the 18th complete with a top hat, file through the foyer and up the front staircase. Since it wasn't a costume party, the hostess felt obligated to investigate who the potential party crasher was. When reaching the top of the stairs, Margareta didn't see the uninvited visitor, but was startled at what she felt when reaching the top step. She recalled the air temperature dropped drastically, as if she had stepped into a walk-in freezer. The startled homeowner hastily and franticly returned to the safety of the party downstairs and decided to sleep on the couch downstairs the next few nights, with a light on. Ghost and paranormal researchers, who have done investigations at the property have concluded the frequent sighting and cold readings usually occur at the front step as if the restless spirit in constantly entering and departing his former home, directly through the front door.

As you can see, Clarke Street is quite active, even to this day. There are almost weekly eyewitness sightings and first-hand accounts of unexplained, possibly other worldly events taking place along this haunted thoroughfare. If you want to have a ghostly experience stay in one of the haunted properties of the Inns of Newport collection. Or join one of the nightly seasonal ghost walks, operated for more than

20 years, by Ghost Tours of Newport, RI. and judge for yourself if Clarke Street qualifies as the "Most Haunted" street in America.

www.ghostsofnewport.com

www.innsofnewport.com

Fans of the popular HBO show, the Gilded Age may recognize Clarke Street as the setting for Season 1, episode 5 "Charity has two functions." Clara Barton is trying to raise funds to start the fledgling Red Cross, in Dansville, New York. Many Clarke Street buildings appear in the episode including the Artillery Company, Clarkeston and Clevland House Inns, and the Meeting House.

4

A Secret Stacked in Stone

Atop one of Newport, Rhode Island's highest points, stands a structure that is perhaps one of the most controversial and mysterious objects in all of the Americas. The first time one lays eyes on the mysterious structure, one cannot help but be awed by the immense size and symmetry of this well-built and sturdy tower. After perusing the object, the mind drifts to the obvious question, what was the purpose for this stone tower to be constructed?

Unfortunately, for those of us that need an instant and decisive answer, there isn't one certainty that arises immediately. Philosophers, scientists, theologians and just about every amateur historian who encounters the mysterious stone tower has their own theory as to the origins of the arched, symmetrical column. Locals and visitors alike have been trying to solve this conundrum for over 300 years. One thing is for sure, it was painstakingly constructed by someone, to serve a specific purpose. Sadly, there seems to be more questions than answers that arise from the mystery tower perched high on the hill.

First of all, let's examine some absolutes, before we delve into the possible reasons for the object's construction. It is most certainly circular and built from local sourced, mostly flat stones, set in mortar, to keep the stones stable and in place. As for the structures main support, there are 8 arched columns of larger, flatter stones, holding up the cylindrical top portion. The curved section of each arch, with the flat stones giving support are somewhat angled toward the ground, also held in place with mortar. Each support archway measures 7 and a half feet from top to bottom and sits on a flattened portion of the hillside. The city of Newport has added a wrought iron fence around the tower, to prevent visitors from climbing inside, but you are certainly close enough to see the entire inside of the cylindrical body of the tower.

A look inside reveals notches carved out of the inside of the structure where it appears crossbeams could be laid and a floor across the beams could have existed at one time. There are also 3 small, square windows, with one facing directly down the hill, toward Newport Harbor. The is also an indentation on the northeast curved section of the upper cylinder, which to the untrained eye, could have been used as a fireplace. The total height of the tower is 24 feet and the width across is 23 feet. That is where the absolutes end, and the theories to the structure's origins begin, with some more plausible than others. Let's examine some of the most popular origins that have evolved over the centuries, and we'll let you draw your own conclusion.

The most romanticized of all the stone tower's possible origins is the Viking or Norse hypothesis and has become interwoven into Newport lore. It is so prevalent in local culture that local businesses have adopted the name and have incorporated it into their logos, including a high-end hotel, a local motor tour company and even a dry cleaner. Even the local high school's nickname is "The Vikings." The origin of the theory came from a Dutch scholar named Carl Christian Rafn, who published a series of letters called Antiquites Americanae in 1837. Rafn concluded that Viking Explorers visited the area in the 11th century and the stone structure was built as a Norse House of Worship. His conclusion was based on some poorly drawn architectural renderings of similar Norse churches from that era in Norway and Denmark. Later, other scholars expounded on this idea adding to hysteria that the tower was indeed of Viking origin. Their conclusion was Norse ships did sail into Narragansett Bay, including the Mount Hope area, which is in nearby Bristol, Rhode Island between 1000 and 1004 A.D. Another argument these theorists use is the tower aligns perfectly to points on a compass, similar to other structures in Northern Europe at the time and certainly something sailors would be familiar with, to use in masonry construction. There have been confirmed voyages of Viking fleets arriving in North America, specifically in Newfoundland, Canada, but architectural digs around and under Newport's stone tower have not revealed any 11th century artifacts that would strongly confirm this possibility.

Another plausible possibility is the towers was constructed as a signaling beacon by a shipwrecked Portuguese navigator named Miguel Corte-Real around 1502. Keep in mind the Portuguese were considered some of the most prolific ocean-going explorers of that time, with Prince Henry the Navigator, funding dozens of trips himself along the African Coast. Pedro Cabral had sailed to Brazil in 1500 and claimed the vast territory for his homeland, so sailing across the Atlantic for the Portuguese was not out of the realm of possibility. Cortes Real may have sailed to the Northeast coast of North America in search of his brother, Gaspar, who was reportedly lost in a storm around 1501 off the coast of Newfoundland. Miguel is thought to have entered Narragansett Bay before becoming wrecked himself. The stone structure could have been erected as a signaling beacon to alert rescuers to his whereabouts. Remember, there is an indentation on the upper level, where a signal fire could be built, inside what looks to be a fireplace. To add more plausibility to this theory, Portuguese artifacts, including a canon and sword were found in nearby Fort Ninigret, in Charlestown, Rhode Island and similar watch towers and beacons do exist on the Portuguese coastline.

Perhaps one of the most bizarre possibilities was floated by author Gavin Menzies in his book, "1421, The Year the Chinese Discovered America."

The author theorizes that Chinese explorer Zheng He constructed the structure as a Lighthouse, to alert other Chinese explorers to the exact location of their new colony. Other evidence Menzies used to fortify his findings is the mortar used to hold the stones together is crushed shells, consistent with Chinese building methods of that time period. Also, the towers dimensions almost perfectly match building dimensions and units found in Ming Dynasty China construction. There was also a European Explorer who sailed through the area around the same time named Giovanni Verrazano, who recorded some interesting findings in his expansive journals. He noted many of the citizens he encountered had a skin tone matching the "color of bronze" and had long dark hair. Verrazano also noted the jewelry they wore was consistent with citizens of the Far East. The tower also matches similar structures located at the time along the Chinese coast as well. However, there is one missing piece of evidence that throws cold water on this possibility. Verrazano was a meticulous record keeper and was super observant and sailed extensively through Narragansett Bay and Newport Harbor and never once mentioned a large stone tower, perched high on one of the highest hillsides. Had such a prominent structure existed in 1421, Verrazano would have written about it extensively, yet it is never mentioned, leaving one to conclude it had not been built yet as of his time in the region.

The most recent possibility was proposed by British writer Andrew Sinclair, who had put forth the hypothesis that the Newport Tower was built by medieval Scottish Templars. The templars, led by Scottish earl Henry Sinclair as part of an alleged voyage to New England about a hundred years before Columbus, were searching for a location to hide their pilfered treasure and riches. The somewhat inexplicable theory argues that the tower's windows align, and measurements are given in code, to point you toward the Kensington rune stone in Minnesota, and the possible location of the "Holy Grail." It is just a short trip to West Central Minnesota, just 502 miles as the crow flies.

Now let's bring it back to earth a bit and talk a little about what is the most likely function of our mysterious stone structure. One thing we can be sure of is the property where the tower is located was once owned by the first colonial governor of the Colony of Rhode Island,

Benedict Arnold. If that name rings a bell, it should, he was the great grandfather of the revolutionary war traitor of the same name. The first Arnold owned a large farm in Newport with a home on Spring Street, in the 1660's, including the property where the tower is located, and the family burial plot is located just down the hill on Pelham Street. There is also evidence that a wooden windmill once stood on the exact location but was blown down during a hurricane in 1675. There is also a similar stone windmill near Arnold's boyhood home in Chesterton, England and Arnold mentions his "Stone Built Windmill" in his will, not once but twice! An extensive archaeological dig in 1949 around the tower unearthed more than 20,000 artifacts including a rusted cleaver, a clay pipe and numerous 17th century coins. There was also extensive carbon dating of the mortar used to hold the tower intact, matching the mortar found in other colonial foundations close to Touro Park, where the tower is located. The findings concluded the mortar was "identical in quality and character" to other 17th century buildings found in the immediate vicinity.

So, if you do visit Newport, make the short walk up the hill from the Harbor front or Thames Street on Mill or Pelham Streets, and see the more than 1 million pounds of fieldstone for yourself. Once you arrive in Touro Park, gaze upon the magnificent stone circular structure, and form your own opinion to its mysterious origin. Most likely, the enduring mystery will never be solved, and rest assured, there are plenty of Newporter's who would like to keep it that way! The never-ending saga is good for business!

Why was this Stone Tower built? Watchtower? Lighthouse? Windmill Base? The truth is no one is actually quite sure...

(Photo courtesy of the author.)

5

America's Royal Family

    September 12th,1953 is one of those dates, which will forever be etched on Newport, Rhode Island's historical timeline. This was the date that fortified the union between 2 of this country's most powerful, wealthy, and politically connected families. The Kennedy clan of Boston would unite with the Auchincloss family from New York, to finalize a plan set in motion by a conniving and ruthless family patriarch years earlier. Joseph P. Kennedy Sr. had for years planned for one of his sons to assume the highest elected post in America, the Presidency. His plan almost became derailed by WWII with the premature death of his oldest son, Joseph Kennedy Jr. in a secret bombing mission over eastern England in 1944. Kennedy Jr. was piloting a B-24 bomber rigged with a high explosive, that once armed, would explode by a timer. The pilotless plane would be guided by remote control over the English Channel to a German U-Boat base in the North Sea. Once

Kennedy armed the timer, the plan was, the airmen would safely parachute out of the flying bomb and glide safely to British soil. Kennedy Jr. never got the chance to ascend to the White House as his father had planned. The bomb detonated prematurely and the heir to the influential Kennedy clan and his co-pilot were killed in the violent explosion.

Joseph Kennedy would turn to another son, John Fitzgerald Kennedy to carry out his plan to finally have a son become President of the United States. John was also a decorated combat veteran, as Captain of the sunken PT. 109, he was able to elude capture by the Japanese while saving some of his surviving crew in the process. After the war, his political career began as a congressman, then was elected as a Massachusetts's Senator in 1952 as the young age of 35. Joseph Kennedy Sr.'s plan was slowing gaining traction, but a storybook marriage would really put the plan in high gear. The Kennedy Patriarch was about to get his wish. That summer, the dashing Congressman, while attending a Georgetown dinner party, was introduced to a young Washington Times Herald photographer through a mutual friend. Her name was Jaqueline Bouvier, a former debutant of the year, she was immediately attracted to the dashing politician. Miss Bouvier certainly checked all the boxes for a wife of a future President of the United States and Joe Kennedy Sr. would certainly agree.

Jaqueline Bouvier was the daughter of Janet and John Vernou Bovier III, otherwise known as "Black Jack" for his dark complexion, heavy drinking, gambling, and playboy lifestyle. After 12 years of marriage Janet had finally had enough and divorced the hard living "Black Jack" to marry a the more stable and deeper pocketed New York stockbroker named Hugh Auchincloss. (Ironically, Jacqueline would marry a man with very similar character traits as her father, in just 12 short years.)

If the Kennedy family was known as political royalty in the United States, the Auchincloss' lineage was very well known and established as titans of American Business with expansive bank accounts to match. Hugh's maternal grandfather was Oliver Burr Jennings, an original partner in Standard Oil with John D. Rockefeller and was worth over 10 million dollars when he passed away, in 1893. Hugh Auchincloss parlayed his family wealth and connections into a successful Brokerage Business, first by purchasing a seat on the "New

York Stock Exchange" then opening a number of Brokerage offices throughout the East Coast of the United States, eventually totaling 16 branches that would bear his and his partners names. Hugh Auchincloss also inherited his family's summer estate, a 28-room ocean front property, built in 1887, known as Hammersmith Farm. After the marriage of Janet and Hugh Auchincloss, young Jaqueline would spend her summers here, developing her love of riding and equestrian skills on the expansive rolling, seaside lower fields of the property.

The day of Holy matrimony finally arrived, September 12, 1953 at The Holy Name of Mary, Our Lady of the Isle Catholic Church, better known locally as St. Mary's. With its founding in 1828, to support the locally burgeoning Irish population, St. Mary's is the oldest Catholic parish in Rhode Island. The current structure dominates a prominent downtown corner, with its unmistakable Gothic Revival architecture and towering spire, St. Mary's has watched over the corner of Spring Street and Memorial Boulevard since 1848.

As you can imagine the union of a Boston political fraternity to a New York City finance and old money oil family would be considered the social event of the decade. To be invited to such a social event would mean you were truly part of business and politics who's who. The actual ceremony, which was slated to begin at 11A.M, jammed the church to the rafters with roughly 800 high-end invitees. Paparazzi and press were stretched along the sidewalk on both sides of St. Mary' clamoring for any view of the wedding party, or the bride and groom themselves.

The marriage ceremony did not go off without a hitch however, as the father of the bride predictably carried on his partying ways throughout the night before the ceremony and into the next morning. "Black Jack" Bouvier was seen drinking and carrying on with his entourage at numerous Newport watering holes well into the night, and when they closed for the night, the party continued at Bouvier's suite at the upscale Hotel Viking, just up the hill from St. Mary's. When word was sent to Jaqueline's mother Janet, about the state of "Black Jack's" condition, she put her foot down. Janet issued a declaration that the still drunk father of the bride was banned from the ceremony so as not to disrupt and disturb his daughter or the ceremony itself. Gracefully, the dignified stepfather Hugh D. Auchincloss, stepped in and walked Jaqueline Bouvier down the aisle, to marry Senator John F. Kennedy.

Massive crowds were hoping for a glimpse of the newly married JFK and Jackie outside St. Mary's Church. (Photo courtesy of JFK presidential library.)

With the union complete at St. Mary's, the reception began at the Auchincloss estate on

Ocean Drive, Hammersmith Farm. The 90+ acre ocean front estate could certainly accommodate more guests than the downtown church, so an estimated 1200 guests attended the post ceremony reception. It was reported the receiving line to congratulate the newly married couple lasted 2 and ½ hours. Party attendees remarked it felt more like a royal coronation than a wedding reception. After the lavish post wedding after party, the Bride and Groom jetted off to Acapulco, Mexico where Jackie realized the wedding vows would be short lived.

The Kennedy Wedding Reception was held at the Auchincloss family estate, Hammersmith Farm along the picturesque Ocean Drive.

(Photo courtesy of JFK presidential library.)

After spending time in Mexico, the newlyweds flew up the coast to Los Angeles to meet up with an old friend and future brother-in-law, Hollywood Star, Peter Lawford. After a shot time JFK asked Jackie if she would head back to Washington D.C. without him. He had some official business to take care of. But Jackie wasn't falling for it, she knew what her husband and wingman Peter Lawford were up to. Jackie's hopes that the vows of marriage would end JFK's seemingly endless lust for new conquests would end, were sadly mistaken.

Now that John Kennedy had what appeared to be the perfect life, married to a former debutante and children on the way, the Kennedy family political machine was full steam ahead. They targeted the 1960 presidential election, and finally fulfilling the family patriarchs, lifelong dream, a son in the White House as President. John Kennedy would win the 1960 presidential election over Republican Richard Nixon by the slimmest of margins, becoming the 35th President of the United States at the young age of 43. Now Jackie hoped as President, JFK would become the responsible husband and family man she had married, however his newfound fame and popularity only added to his womanizing and brazen behavior and would even carry out affairs, right under his wife's nose in the White House.

JFK's most famous mistress was none other than famous Hollywood starlet, Marilyn Monroe, who was introduced to the president by fellow Hollywood actor, Peter Lawford. The Hollywood starlet become so smitten with the handsome yet married Commander in Chief, she was calling the White House switchboard constantly, trying to speak to her former lover. The President was either too busy or disinterested in speaking with Marilyn and dispatched his brother Robert, the current Attorney General, to California to deal with "the problem." Soon after this visit, America's best-known starlet, was found dead in her Brentwood home, from a reported Barbiturate overdose and probable suicide. However, rumors were running rampant throughout Tinseltown that Marilyn was preparing to talk and reveal she was having simultaneous affairs, with the President, his brother Bobby and another famous Hollywood actor, Frank Sinatra. Had Marilyn spilled the beans, it would have catastrophic to the president's family man image, and she had to be silenced. Did the Kennedy's and Sinatra use their vast underworld connections to have Marilyn

Monroe silenced? That is one secret that sadly has gone to their respected graves and will remain one of Hollywood's enduring mysteries.

The President would spend a lot of time in Newport during the summer of 1962, earning Hammersmith Farm the nickname, The Summer White House. JFK was an avid sailor from his childhood days growing up in nearby Hyannisport on Cape Cod and felt at ease on the water. He also had longtime Democratic Senator Claiborne Pell around town, as a good friend, a staunch ally and perhaps as a buddy to grab a drink or 2 with at Bailey's Beach Club! The president was keenly interested in the America's Cup Yacht races held that summer in and around Newport Harbor and Narragansett Bay. The president would be seen frequently on viewing boats to get up close and personal with the race action and far away from the prying eyes of the press corp. JFK was also frequently seen walking the along the shore at the ultra-private beach club, The Spouting Rock Beach Association with his young son, John- John. Sadly, the summer of 1962 would be the last peaceful summer the president would get to experience. With the close call of a nuclear war with Russia and the Cuban Missile crisis in October 1962, going forward the President would have to deal with numerous crises', both foreign, domestic and at home, moving forward.

By late 1962, Jaqueline has grown weary of her husband's long list of mistresses and was openly discussing leaving Washington for good, with her children in tow, and moving back in with her parents at their stately Newport Manor, Hammersmith Farm. But JFK needed to keep up his family man image and public persona, with a re-election bid upcoming shortly, he promised his loyal wife, his days of messing around with the likes of Marilyn Monroe were behind him. He did neglect to mention however, he would still be carrying on extra marital affairs with Janet Exner, the girlfriend of Chicago mob boss Sam Giancana, actress Angie Dickinson and Washington D.C. socialite Mary Pinchot Meyer, to name a few. There were also a pair of voluptuous White House Secretaries that the Secret Service nicknamed Fiddle and Faddle, who would accompany the President as he swam in the white house pool. The president claimed these almost daily sessions were needed as therapy for his ailing, sometimes debilitating back problems, while Jaqueline would be attending to their children upstairs in the White House residence.

By 1963 the Kennedy Administration was pushing for a Civil Rights Bill on the home front and increased tensions in Vietnam over communism spreading throughout Southeast Asia dominated the foreign agenda. Closer to home, the President was planning to spend more time, the following summer in Newport, and had made plans to rent the adjacent mansion to Hammersmith Farm, the Armsea Estate. Locals joked it was perhaps to stash his stable of mistresses while visiting the in-laws next door.

Regrettably, the president would never get the opportunity to spend another glorious day in the City by the Sea. His life was cut short by a lone assassin's bullet, if you believe the Warren Report, November 22,1963 while riding in an open limousine in Dallas, Texas. With John Kennedy's death, the so-called story book presidency "Camelot" came to a premature end.

The Kennedy mystique was largely a creation of his well-connected father, his outstanding charisma and charm along with the assistance of some powerful, yet sinister allies. Ironically, it was some of the same elements that made him so popular, perhaps along with his own sense of invincibility, which combined to create so many enemies, that also wanted to bring him down.

President Kennedy spent a good deal of time at Hammersmith Farm during his presidency, earning the seaside estate the nickname the "Summer White House."

(Photo courtesy of Life magazine, public domain.)

6

Leap of Faith

Most likely, if you have driven to Newport in the past, you have crossed the Newport, Pell Bridge. The impressive local landmark is named for Senator Claiborne Pell, a 6 term Statesman who hailed from the City by the Sea. The impressive span over the east passage of Narragansett Bay offers stunning views of the downtown waterfront, Fort Adams, and Goat Island to the south. A Glance to the north you'll see the expansive Naval Station, The Naval War College, Miantonomi Hill and the WW I memorial. The Bridge was completed in 1969 at a cost of over 50 million dollars and is the longest suspension bridge in all of New England at just over 2 miles in length. The span connects Conanicut Island and the town of Jamestown to Aquidneck Island and replaced a ferry service between the Islands that ran since the 17th century. The prominent towers soar 250 feet over the bay with the roadbed an impressive 215 feet at its zenith above the saltwater below. The Pell Bridge is without a doubt the lifeline to Newport tourism and commercial traffic.

The thousands of cars, trucks and buses carrying hopefully excited tourists and visitors unlikely to know the sinister and dark history incorporated with the tallest structure in the area. Perhaps you have noticed the signs as you start the climb up the incline, that if you are depressed, there are options. Call this number and speak to Samaritans of Rhode Island for help, the sign implores those who may be considering ending their lives. Sadly, the towering structure offers this option to those considering it. During the last 9 years alone, there have been at least 27 recorded deaths by suicide at the region's bridges. The trend has become so rampant that state legislators have introduced bills to install netting as a suicide prevention to the 4 area crossings. There is also a mystery that endures to this day, so baffling it continues to confound law enforcement and bounty hunters more almost 30 years after it occurred. And it was all centered at the top the Newport Bridge!

What started out as a fun night out for dinner, turned into a life altering experience for Warwick's Adam Emery and his wife Elena. On the evening of August 1, 1990, Adam Emery, his wife, Elena, his sister-in-law Maria, and her husband, Ronnie, were sitting in Emery's 1985 black Thunderbird in a parking lot outside a restaurant in Rocky Point when the T-Bird car was struck by another car, which sped away. The 2 couples were in hot pursuit eventually getting the suspected car to pull over and Emery confronted the driver with a knife. 20-year-old Jay Bass and a passenger, refuted Emery's claims, they weren't at the Rocky Point restaurant and the incensed Emery had a case of mistaken identity. Then Bass put the car in reverse, trying to move away, Emery screamed for the accused driver to stop. When Bass did not, the enraged Emery plunged the knife in the young man's chest, and he died from his wounds a short time later at Rhode Island Hospital. As it turns out, Bass' car was not the vehicle that struck Emery's T-Bird based on paint matching by the Rhode Island State Police. Adam Emery had killed an innocent man. However, Emery insisted that he killed Bass in self-defense, but a jury disagreed, and was found guilty of second-degree murder on November 10, 1993, ironically his 31st birthday.

For some bizarre reason, the judge allowed him to remain free on bail pending formal sentencing a month later, setting off an unexplained series of events, we still don't have the answers to. At 3:00 PM, Adam left the courthouse with Elena, and a half hour later, the Emerys showed up at a local sporting goods store to purchase sweatsuits, athletic socks, and 80 pounds of strap-on exercise weights.

After the brief shopping spree, the couple was seen, calmly dining at a local Burger King. Witnesses said the pair seemed perfectly fine, relaxed and nothing appeared out of the ordinary. But that later that afternoon, Emery started his devious plan, one he hoped would lead to his freedom. At 4:50 PM, eyewitnesses recalled seeing the Emerys on the walkway of the bridge, but perhaps they got cold feet and by 5:15 P.M. the convicted murderer and his wife drove away. Two hours after, their car was found back on the Newport bridge, but what happened after that is still a mystery today, nearly 30 years later. Just before 7PM, their abandoned car was found on the Newport Bridge; the engine was running, and the lights were on. Neatly folded clothes were found on the back seat. On the front seat there was cash, cut-up credit cards, and Adam's driver's license. After an examination of a video taken in court, Emery whispered to his wife Elena, "We will do what we originally said. You promised me. We should have done this before." Had the couple entered a suicide pact? Based on the evidence found that evening, it certainly seemed like the case. The Emery's wanted authorities to believe they jumped hand in hand off the Pell Bridge and into eternity forever. Time to close the book on the Murder of Jason Bass and the joint suicide of the Emery's. Or was it???

Almost immediately, police, detectives and Coast Guard combed the area for clues to the couple's disappearance and of course to locate bodies in the water. Despite law enforcement's best efforts, no bodies were recovered. Perhaps the weight belts the couple had purchased at the sporting goods store earlier that afternoon sank them deep into the muddy bottom of Narragansett Bay. Truly a baffling end to sad and senseless tragedy for all the families involved. In August of 1994, the authorities finally got a clue as to what may have occurred that fateful night. A fisherman working in the bay found two human leg bones in his net. Clinging to one was a fragment of a sock that was identical to those purchased by Adam and Elena. Authorities compared the DNA sample from the bone with DNA samples of both Elena's mother and sister. It was an identical match. Then a few weeks later, the watery grave had given up another grim piece of evidence. A skull recovered from the east passage of the bay in another fisherman's net and was positively identified as that of Elena Emery. Yet there is still no sign of her husband Adam. Rumors began to surface that Adam Emery wasn't actually dead. People claimed to have seen him in Connecticut and then in Florida. So, what actually happened on the Bridge that fateful November night in 1993? Our guess is Adam never planned to commit suicide at all. It was all a ruse to fake his death and slip out of the country and live the rest of his life abroad. He and his wife most likely had a suicide pact. At the top of the bridge, they held hands and counted to 3 to jump, 1, 2, 3! Adam fooled Elena and they would jump together hand in hand. While she plunged to her death in the icy water below, Adam remained on the bridge and slipped into the night...Never to be seen again.

The F.B.I. still considers Adam Emery a fugitive, almost 30 years after his disappearance. Despite being featured on Nightline, Unsolved Mysteries, and other crime finder TV shows, the wanted escapee has never been found. The most prominent rumor was Emery fled the country and has been on the run in Italy ever since. And chances are after reading this tale, you will never look at the Newport Pell Bridge again the same way.

Did Adam and Elena Emery jump hand in hand off the Newport, Pell Bridge? Or was it an elaborate hoax to fate his death?

(Photo courtesy of the author.)

7

Conspiracies on the High Seas

Far be it from rich and powerful titans of industry to bend the rules in their favor. That also may be the case when it came to their expensive hobby, Yacht racing and their quest for the America's Cup Trophy. The prestigious Cup was first captured in 1851, when the regatta was called the 100 Guinea Cup, around the Isle of Wight of the south Coast of England. The lone entrant from the New York Yacht club, a schooner named "America" out raced 15 British challengers, and the America's Cup was born. The New York Yacht club would retain this prestigious trophy for the next 132 years, albeit at times not showing the best of sportsmanship to their challengers. The rules stated that whoever holds the cup is permitted to select the venue as well as the size of the Yachts participating. There is no doubt the N.Y.Y.C. would do everything in their power to retain the "Auld Mug." Another advantage the American team would enjoy for years was certainly a distinct home field advantage. Opposing crews were required to sail their race boats across the Atlantic, enduring a treacherous and grueling crossing, even before competing in the race. The refrain "Britania rules the waves, But America waves the rules!" was a popular refrain from opposing owners and crews for more than 100 years. But all is fair in Love and Yachting!

Keep in mind, the quadrennial event was not always held off the shore of Newport. Initially the New York Yacht club would hold their cup challenges closer to home, off the New Jersey coast near Sandy Hook. During the decades of the 1870's 80's and 90's, the New York Yacht Club held a huge advantage thanks to a local yacht designer. Their secret weapon was an innovative Yacht builder named Nathanael Herreshoff from nearby Bristol, Rhode Island. He was known to innovate with new materials like aluminum and created better lighter, more aerodynamic hull designs. One of Hereshoff's most famous Yachts was the Columbia, which easily bested Sir Thomas Lipton's Shamrock to win the 1899 America's Cup. Sir Thomas Lipton, owner of the world renown tea company, would be defeated in the next 3 challenges as well, spending untold millions of dollars, just for the right to hoist a 3-foot silver trophy. He would never earn this right, however.

The America's Cup would finally arrive in Newport in 1930. The New York Yacht club moved their clubhouse to the City by the Sea, and the racing conditions were thought to be more conducive to competing offshore. The currents and tides around Sandy Hook, New Jersey were at times unpredictable, not to mention the high volume of shipping traffic in and out of nearby New York Harbor. From 1930 onward Newport would inexorably be linked with the America's Cup. 1930 would be Sir Thomas Lipton's last go at the elusive cup, by was easily brushed aside by a hometown entry, Harold Stirling Vanderbilt from the Marble House. Vanderbilt had a cutting edge designed "J Boat" and captained the "Enterprise" to a commanding victory. J class boats were considered the Grande Dames of America's Cup Racing, with their more than 100-foot-long hulls with masts rising over 80 feet. The Enterprise was cutting edge for its day with an all-aluminum mast. The challenger, the Shamrock V, was a traditional, lumbering all wooden yacht and was no match for the innovatively designed Enterprise. Sir Thomas Lipton was defeated again and died shortly thereafter in 1931, heartbroken he never was able to raise the America's Cup.

There was a new challenger to join the chase in 1934, with famous British airplane designer and industrialist, Sir Thomas Sopwith, best known for his WWI design the Camel. The results would be the same, however, as part time Newporter, Harold S. Vanderbilt continued the winning streak in 1934 and again in 1937. After the last cup victory, the races would be paused indefinitely with Hitler's annexation of Austria, and subsequent invasions of Czechoslovakia and Poland in Europe, the winds of war would end the prestigious Yacht race for nearly 2 decades. With the pause came an end to the short-lived J class boat era.

Hometown hero Harold Stirling Vanderbilt, 3-time winner of the prestigious America's Cup.

(Photo courtesy of America's Cup yachting museum.)

By 1956, the war was a distant memory, so the New York Yacht club decided it was time to restart the America's Cup challenges. There was one major change involved with the relaunch of the races, the style of boats would now be a smaller, more cost-effective style called 12 meters. The 12 meters were much smaller and nimbler than the previous style, the monstrous J Boats.

The 1962 races drew a lot of attention to Newport, with President Kennedy frequently in town, often seen watching the action from viewing boats offshore. 1962 was also the 1st year the challenger for the cup was from Australia, but still the yacht from down under was no match for the home team's entry, Weatherly.

1977 was another memorable America's Cup summer, mostly for the captain of the 12 meter Courageous and self-proclaimed "Mouth of the South" Ted Turner. He was so drunk and obnoxious he managed to get himself thrown out of and banned indefinitely from the Yachties favorite waterfront watering hole, The Black Pearl. Turner later bragged he wandered down the street to local favorite restaurant Salas and dined without an issue on their famous oriental spaghetti.

1983 was a pivotal year for the history of the America's Cup at least as far as Newport was concerned. Australian yacht owner Alan Bond was back with a vengeance after feeling slighted and embarrassed by Turner at the previous challenge. The egotistical Bond had a secret weapon up his sleeve with his newly designed entry, Australia II. It had a winged keel, that was so cutting edge, it was wrapped in a tarp, so the competition couldn't see its design. One morning at 2am. the Australian boat's security team, chased away a frogman seen under the secretive winged keel, no doubt trying to get a sneak peek at the innovative design and share it with the American side.

The American's yacht Liberty with Captain Dennis Connor at the helm, got off to a strong start, winning the first 2 races, but the innovative winged keel design proved to be too fast, and the Australian won 4 of the next 5 matches. On September 26th, 1983, the longest winning streak in modern sports history finally ended. After 132 years, the New York Yacht club lost to the Royal Perth Yacht Club. However, multiple rumors would spread on how the Australia II was able to defeat, the highly favored Liberty. During the final, decisive race, Liberty had a lead, closing toward the finish line off of Brenton Point State Park. American captain ordered an amateurish maneuver, causing the sail on Liberty to luff, basically losing power and forward speed, and allowing the challenger Australia II to pass the Liberty and advance across the finish line. Local whispers grew louder that Captain Conner let Australia win the final race to finally wrestle the "Auld Mug" out of the hands of the New York Yacht Club, to eventually get the cup to the West Coast of the United States. The 1987 America's Cup was easily won back by Captain Dennis Conner, off the Freemantle, Australia coast, with a shutout of the host country, 4-0. The America's Cup now headed to the west coast and the San Diego Yacht Club. It is highly improbable the cup, will ever return to Newport and its original owner, The Newport Yacht Club. The costs involved make America's Cup yacht racing only attainable to the super wealthy, literally the top 1 percent of the top 1 percenters. Part time local Newport resident and property owner, Larry Ellison of the Oracle Corporation is one of those people. He briefly held the America's Cup trophy in 2010 with his yacht Oracle but was affiliated with the Golden Gate Yacht Club in San Fransisco. Apparently, Ellison had applied for membership to the stoic New York Yacht Club but was denied. He was considered new money apparently and too nouveau riche for the N.Y.Y.C. standards… OOPs. Either way, 132 years is a pretty good run though and most certainly that streak will never be matched.

It is almost impossible to calculate the amount of money spent, trying to capture the "Auld Mug" a trophy standing just over 3 and a half feet tall, weighing just over 30 pounds.

(Photo courtesy of America's Cup yachting museum.)

8

U.S.S. Bennington

If you have ever visited Newport, Rhode Island, and have traveled to expansive Fort Admas State Park, you have likely seen the signs for the U.S.S. Bennington memorial. If you wind up the curvy driveway, past the Eisenhower house you will be awarded with fantastic views of the east passage of Narragansett Bay, the island of Jamestown, the Rose Island Lighthouse, and the aforementioned Newport Pell Bridge. A quick scan of the expansive lawn will reveal a squared hedgerow which inside contains a small military cemetery, mostly for servicemen stationed at the adjacent Fort Adams. Directly on the outside, close to the bay, and next to an access road called Lincoln Drive, you will see a waist high granite and brass memorial surrounded by a neatly kept stone circle. On the brass plaque is inscribed the names of the 103 officers and sailors who perished that day, May 26th,1954 just south of

Newport, along the Rhode Island Coast. But what happened that fateful day is still up for debate and even now, shrouded in mystery.

The U.S.S. Bennington was launched from the New York Naval Shipyard in 1944 and was almost immediately assigned to a task force with other aircraft carriers in the South Pacific, specifically around the island of Okinawa, a Japanese stronghold. The Carriers were so close to mainland Japan, their planes were able to carry out bombing missions over Tokyo and enemy airfields on the island of Kyushu. On April 7th,1945, the Bennington's torpedo planes participated in an attack on the Japanese Battleship Yamato, eventually sinking it, and further crippling an already depleted Japanese Navy. After WW II ended, the U.S.S. Bennington continued operations around the Japanese home islands in support of occupation forces. The carrier's airmen conducted routine patrols as well as searches for internment camps containing Allied prisoners of war. That duty lasted until September 1945, at which time the U.S.S. Benington triumphantly entered Tokyo Bay.

After the war, Bennington was idle for almost four years, but was about to be re-born, just in time for the cold war. In October 1950, the carrier was moved to the New York Naval Shipyard to receive much needed updates. Over the next two years, she underwent a transformation which modernized the carrier to modern-day military standards. The flight deck was strengthened and widened to accommodate 1950's era jet aircraft and the installation of catapults, internal airplane elevators and a pitched flight deck to assist in rapid take offs. By October 1952, Big Benn, as she was affectionally nicknamed by her crew, was ready for a new life as an attack aircraft carrier and received a new designation, CVA-20.

The U.S.S. Bennington's new life as an attack carried got off to a rough start, however. During a training mission, off the Florida coast an explosion below deck rocked the Bennington on April 27th,1953 killing 11 sailors on board. The Bennington limped into Guantanamo Bay, Cuba for repairs. A subsequent inquiry by Naval investigators could not determine the cause of the explosion. Were they covering up a design flaw, that would once again rear its ugly head and only cause more death and destruction? That is what some of the crew of the Bennington felt and sadly their fears would be realized, just a little over 1 year later.

May 26th, 1954, started early onboard the U.S.S. Bennington, steaming off the Southern Coast of Rhode Island, on a clear and unusually calm day at sea. By 6am. flight operations were well underway as the newly renovated carrier was launching its fighter force as pilots were doing their Aircraft Carrier qualifications. The Bennington had been recently assigned to the Quonset Naval Station, directly west of Newport Narragansett Bay. The first sign of trouble was with the newly installed hydraulic catapult, with a malfunction on the first launch attempted on the starboard launcher. From that point forward, all flight launches would take place on the port catapult. By 6:10 am. there was another sign of trouble, with smoke being reported in a forward compartment. At 06:11am. there was a violent explosion on the flight deck, which involved the forward third of the ship. Most eyewitnesses said there were two more explosions, even more powerful than the first, below in the catapult compartment. General Quarters were sounded, and the orders spread quickly and with panic over the ship's loudspeaker... "This Is Not a Drill!" Some sailors onboard thought they were being attacked, perhaps by an enemy torpedo or even a bomb. Fire crews were dispatched below the flight deck, toward the front of the carrier and were shocked at what they found. All the men in the forward catapult room were dead from the force of the blast. Other survivors literally had their clothes burned off from the extreme heat generated from the fire. And flames were still burning uncontrolled in the forward compartments of the ship. It took almost a full hour, after the series of explosions, to finally extinguish the dangerous internal blazes. By 10 am. the ship's sick bay and its 60 beds were filled with wounded and dying sailors. To make matters worse, one of the 3 onboard physicians was killed in the blast and the growing number of casualties was quickly overwhelming the medical staff.

With smoke still pouring out of the lower decks, Captain Raborn turned the Bennington north, back into Narragansett Bay and steamed toward Newport as fast as the badly damaged carrier could muster. All aircraft that could take off without a catapult assist, were launched from the flight deck to clear space onboard for a daring shipboard rescue, in an attempt to save the critically wounded. One of the Navy's newest aircraft arrived, the helicopter, first transporting urgently needed physicians and corpsmen to tend to the wounded. Then the helicopters would turn back north, eventually flying 64 seriously burned crewmen to the nearby Naval Hospital. Perhaps the only positive outcome of this horrific day was the effectiveness of helicopter in a carrier borne rescue mission. (A prelude to the Vietnam conflict.)

The Bennington would eventually return to the New York Naval Shipyard for repairs, and they were quite extensive. There was notable damage as far down as 3 decks below the flight deck. The most severe structural damage was found in the forward hangar deck, with up to 4-inch bulges, facing upward. The explosion was so powerful, it forced 2-and-a-half-inch special treated steel armor to bulge and bubble up to 4 inches outward. Naval engineers remarked they had never seen such structural damage from an internal blast.

A Naval Board of Inquiry did a full investigation of Bennington's explosion and ruled out sabotage, crew error and exonerated Captain Raborn. The likely cause was a hydraulic fluid leak on the starboard catapult, that eventually became so overheated by a buildup of hot air and gases, it had no other option than to literally blow its top! The leaking hydraulic fluid was also highly flammable, exacerbating the ferocity of the blast. One very troubling pronouncement from the board of injury noted for many years, the Navy was aware of potential fire and explosion risks associated with the hydraulic catapults. Of course, there was never a severe incident, until May 26,1954. But at that point it was too late, 103 officers and sailors were dead and more than 200 were wounded. All due to a leaky hydraulic catapult, which the Navy admitted they knew could be catastrophic.

By the late 1950's most of Worlds Navies and their respective Aircraft Carriers, were switching to a safer and more powerful catapult system, which used steam from ship's boilers to launch aircraft and assist with landings with a hook and wire system. The hydraulic mechanisms and the highly flammable oil and fluid were a thing of the past. Modern Aircraft carriers use what's called the Electromagnetic Aircraft Launch System or EMALS. EMALS reduces stress on airframes because they can be accelerated more gradually to takeoff speed than steam-powered catapults. EMALS weighs less, occupies less space, requires less maintenance and manpower, is more reliable, uses less energy and best of all much safer for Naval Personnel. Sadly the U.S.S. Bennington didn't have access to this kind of technology during it early tours of duty.

The U.S.S. Bennington with a full flight deck, off the coast of Vietnam, 1965.

(Photo courtesy of U.S. Navy archives.)

The U.S.S. Bennington was back at sea by the 1960's and saw extensive duty during the Vietnam conflict and was the recovery ship for the unmanned Apollo 4 space craft after it splashed down at sea in 1967. But by 1970, the

Bennington was retired to a Navy Shipyard in Washington State, eventually decommissioned, and eventually sold for scrap in 1994. After 26 years of tumultuous, yet faithful service, Big Benn had finally reached the end of the line and the U.S.S Bennington was stricken from the Naval Registry of active Vessels.

When the Navy selects names for a new ship, they may want to consider something besides Bennington. You are now familiar with the unfortunate incident that took place aboard the Aircraft Carrier, but did you know this ship's namesake also had a similar, catastrophic experience as well? The first incarnation of the Bennington was a steel hulled gun boat launched in 1890. On July 21st ,1905 in San Diego, California, the 1st Bennington suffered a boiler explosion, tragically killing 66 men and injuring nearly everyone else on board. It is probably just a coincidence but let's hope the Navy permanently retires the name U.S.S Bennington. May they all rest in peace!

9

The Restless Spirit of Rose Island

The is a small Island just under the south side of the Newport Pell Bridge, called Rose Island. During the summer season day trippers can visit and the only way to arrive is via the Jamestown Ferry. The restored Lighthouse on the Island offers guests the opportunity to spend the night and even perform the tasks of a 19th century Lighthouse keeper. Keep in mind that if you accept this task, you may have an unseen assistant, monitoring your every move! And once the last ferry departs for the evening, there is no way to leave the Island!

The need for a Lighthouse on Rose Island was growing in the mid-1860's at a time when the state of Rhode Island was expanding commerce and shipping traffic was increasing on Narragansett Bay. Steamship companies were ramping up routes during this time ferrying seasonal passengers and freight in the bay between Newport, New York, and Boston. The lighthouse was built on the southwest bastion of old Fort Hamilton, a revolutionary war era battery, and its fixed red light was first shone over lower Narragansett Bay in January 1870.

But by 1970, the Rose Island Lighthouse, was no longer deemed necessary as an aid to navigation, and was decommissioned by the U.S. Coast Guard. In the mid 1980's a group of avid lighthouse fans were able to convince the federal government to deed control of the Lighthouse to the city of Newport, with plans to save the abandoned Light Station. With the help of private donations and fundraisers, they were able to restore the Rose Island Lighthouse to its 1870's glory. On August 7, 1993, the lighthouse restoration was complete and for the first time in over 20 years, the Rose Island Lighthouse was back in operation! The light was re-ignited from the Light tower, 48 feet above the waters of Narragansett Bay as a visual aid to guide ships under the Newport Bridge and up into the bay. The Rose Island Light is currently considered a Private Aid to Navigation, sanctioned by the U.S. Coast Guard, but maintained and operated by the Rhode Island Lighthouse Federation.

So, if you decide to spend a night, or even a week as the lighthouse keeper, plan way ahead of time. The rooms at the Rose Island Lighthouse books months or even years in advance, even with the restless sprit or spirits, that still inhabit the island.

Reserve early if you plan to stay at the Rose Island Lighthouse. But remember, you may not be alone! (Photo courtesy of the author.)

The popular TV show Ghost Hunters and The Atlantic Paranormal Society (TAPS) led by Jason and Grant, had heard the rumors of the hauntings on Rose Island for years. In 2010, they hopped the ferry and decided to spend the night and see for themselves, bringing along a camera crew and their ghost hunting apparatus. They would not be disappointed, as almost immediately between the kitchen and dining room, the duo sees a shadow and hears some bizarre noises moving between the rooms. Overnight guests of the lighthouse have reported seeing a woman in a blue dress wandering this area of the property. Other members of the team investigate the lightroom, where numerous sightings have occurred and ghost hunters believe the spirit of the longest serving keeper, Charles Curtis, still keeps watch. The team in the lightroom is startled when an access door suddenly closes, striking one of the investigators and they immediately flee to the relative safety of the lower level. But perhaps the most intriguing evidence of paranormal activity is recorded outside, next to an abandoned barracks of the 18th century Fort

Hamilton. The barracks once served a quarantine location for those suffering from cholera in nearby Newport. Sadly, many of those souls suffering from the highly contagious disease, took their last breaths there, never to return to the mainland. A bright white light was seen by numerous members of the TAPS team clinging to an exterior wall of the barracks and then disappearing inside the decaying structure. Upon later investigation and review of a video, a thermal imaging camera picked up a figure moving away from the building and an infrared camera captured a flash of light at the exact same moment. The normally skeptical investigators cannot offer an explanation as to what they had captured. They reviewed an old photograph of Lighthouse keeper, Charles Curtis. It was nearly identical to a reflection captured inside the lighthouse keeper's quarters that very evening. Based on the evidence acquired from fist hand experience, the TAPS team concluded, Rose Island was the most haunted location they had even seen!

Does the restless spirit of the longest tenured Lighthouse Keeper, Charles Curtis, still wander Rose Island?

(Photo courtesy of New England Lighthouse Museum.)

10

The House on a Rock

One of the most unique summer homes you will even encounter, is just a stone's throw from Conanicut Island and the town of Jamestown. The property is called "Clingstone" which of course has a double meaning. The name implies it is a peach of a home with an unbelievable view. It also signifies it is literally perched on an outcropping on Narragansett Bay known as "The Dumplings." Despite its precarious location, Clingstone is a survivor, and miraculously was able to weather the most powerful hurricane the east coast of the United States has ever experienced, in 1938. Even more remarkably, a former owner of the property, weathered the storm inside "The House on a Rock."

Clingstone was built in 1905 for J.S. Wharton, a wealthy and influential industrialist from Philadelphia. His uncle was Joseph Wharton, founder of the prestigious school of business at the University of Pennsylvania.

(Photo courtesy of the author with an assist from Drone Photos RI.)

J.S. Wharton chose the precarious location to build Clingstone after the town of Jamestown, and the federal government demolished his first summer home, to re-build a revolutionary war era fortification, now called Fort Weatherill. With the assistance of renowned artist, William

Trost Richards, the layout evolved into a three-story 23-room 10,000-square-foot shingle-style cottage. The design system of heavy mill-type framing was intended to withstand hurricane-force winds. The unique design would be severely tested, September 21st, 1938, when the storm of the century unexpectedly and suddenly appeared over Narragansett Bay, literally knocking on the door of Clingstone and much of the east coast of the United States.

September 21st, 1938 started as an unseasonably warm, slightly overcast fall New England day with only a slight breeze. No one could have imagined mother nature's fury was just a few hours away from being unleashed along the coast. The U.S. weather bureau was well aware of a monster hurricane, in the Atlantic, and issued a hurricane warning for Miami, Florida on September 19th. The hurricane never made landfall there however and forecasters assumed it had been caught in the Jetstream and was headed safely out to sea, but tragically this was not the case. September 21st was the highest tide of the entire year and high-pressure area over the Eastern United States and another at sea, prevented the storm from spinning out to sea. This climatic condition acted as a right of way, directing the storm on a long, straight northerly course up the Atlantic coast. Keep in mind, 1930's forecasters were literally flying blind, relying on radio dispatches from ships at sea as well as barometer readings from land-based weather stations. The technology of Doppler radar to track these killer storms was still decades in the future. What we know now, the massive 500-mile-wide hurricane, with Category 5 wind speeds, was paralleling the Atlantic coast, with eastern Connecticut and Rhode Island in its sights.

The first landfall for this massive storm, was the eastern end of Long Island, New York with 100+ mile per hour winds, lashing the beaches there, just after 2pm. By 3pm the storm had engulfed much of tiny Block Island, capsizing 35 of the 50 vessels of the local fishing fleet. The storm was heading on a Northerly track at such a rapid speed, residents in the hurricanes path had no time to prepare. The killer storm was moving at an unprecedented rate of speed at over 70 miles an hour was about to exacerbate the highest tide of the entire year, certainly a recipe for disaster. The rapid velocity of the approaching maelstrom negated New England's best defense against massive hurricanes. The cold water of the Northern Atlantic historically saps the energy from these powerful storms, however in this case, it moved so fast, the last line of defense did not have time to take effect. The unprotected coastline of Southern New England, was about to feel the brunt of the "Storm of the Century!"

The narrow island where Jamestown is located was directly in the hurricane's path, and sadly it wasn't spared any of the storm's rage and ferocity. By late afternoon, winds and waves were picking up, so school authorities, out of an abundance of caution, closed the island's elementary school and sent the children home. When the 8 remaining students and the bus driver, Norman Caswell reached Mackerel Cove, a low-lying beach and causeway which connects the North and South sections of the Island, the waves were already splashing over the road. As Casewell inched the bus through the wind driven waves, a surge hit, stalling the bus about halfway across the now flooded beach road, and it immediately started filling with seawater. Caswell told the children to form a human chain, then opened the bus door, instructing the frightened children to hang on to each other tight, while trying to make it across to high ground on the west side. Waiting on the other side was Joe Matoes, a local resident, who had 4 children on the bus. Matoes himself narrowly escaped drowning minutes earlier as he attempted to drive across the engulfed roadway, his car was swept away by the rising tide and had to swim back to shore. As Matoes watched in horror, another massive wave struck the chain of schoolchildren, sweeping them north into the bay. Only the bus driver Norman Caswell and another student named Clayton Chellis would survive.

Tragically, 6 Jamestown school children, passengers on this bus, would be swept away by the powerful storm surge from the deadly 1938 hurricane. (Photo courtesy of New England Hurricane Hunters.)

Ironically, Clayton Chellis, who would proudly serve his country during WWII as a member of the U.S. Navy, would die from drowning off the Island of Saipan, in the south pacific, in 1946.

Just west of Conanicut Island, stood a light house called Whale Rock, standing as a beacon at the treacherous west passage entrance of Narragansett Bay since 1882. It was a sparkplug style Lighthouse, literally built on top of a stone pedestal, above a rocky outcropping. Tragically, it was no match for the estimated 15-foot-high storm surge, crashing through the bay that afternoon. The intense waves literally ripped Whale Rock Light off its base, killing the lighthouse keeper, Walter Eberle, who was stranded inside when the expected hurricane struck.

Mrs. Wharton was relaxing in Clingstone when the storm hit her house on the rock. The monster hurricane had arrived so rapidly and without warning, area residents had no choice but to shelter in place and pray they would survive the onslaught. Clingstone, with its precarious location, was under assault from the sea with 15 + foot storm surges with sustained winds estimated at over 120+ miles per hour. When the winds finally subsided, Clingstone, thanks to its sturdy construction, survived the assault, but the swimming pool, tennis court as well as the long causeway connecting it to Jamestown were gone. Mrs. Wharton was so shaken and terrified from her experience inside Clingstone during the hurricane, she vowed to never return. True to her word, Mrs. Wharton would never return and the house on the rock was abandoned for decades.

The impact of the storm was almost hard to comprehend. It could certainly be measured in dollars. Total damages were $306 million, which equals roughly $18 billion in today's money. The phycological damage would be hard to measure however and people who survived the terrifying day still reference it as one they will never forget, most likely traumatized forever. If they were lucky enough to survive the storm, the next day's sunrise would reveal an almost unrecognizable landscape. Almost 700 people perished from the storm, with more than 100 in Rhode Island. Jamestown would quickly construct a bridge, to connect it to the Mainland of Rhode Island, as an escape route in case another killer hurricane threatened the area. Train travel between Boston and New York was disrupted for months as crews struggled to clear the tracks and rebuild washed out rail lines. Entire beach communities were literally wiped off the map from the high winds and storm surge, never to be rebuilt. Beaches and coastal dunes that were formed over 1000's of years, disappeared overnight. The force of the hurricane also rendered hundred-year-old nautical charts obsolete, with the closing of channels and inlets along the coast, while opening new ones. Downtown Providence, Rhode Island endured up to 13 feet of flood water in the downtown area. The city would build massive hurricane barriers along the south side of the city, with closable flood doors, in an effort to prevent devastating flood water from inundating the city again. The damage to property was devastating with more than 57,000 buildings destroyed or damaged and roughly 2,500 boats sunk.

Newport did not survive the storm unscathed, especially along the coast. The pavilion of the upscale Bailey's Beach was literally picked up and placed in the middle of Ocean Drive, and a nearby Coast Guard Station was smashed to pieces. The south end of the Cliff walk was seriously damaged and some of the walkway's stone walls were overturned by the powerful waves. Remnants of these walls still lay in pieces and the ruble can still been seen to this day along the path. The biggest blow was suffered at Newport's Easton's Beach where a large amusement park stood. The hugely popular oceanfront park featured a large wooden Roller Coaster, a Massive Ferris Wheel, and the always popular Carousel. By the morning of September 22nd, 1938, they were all gone, as if a petulant child had grown tired of their playthings, and brushed them violently aside, as if they never existed. Regrettably, the Amusement Park would never be rebuilt. As for the house on a rock, it would sit empty and in disrepair until 1961 when it was purchased by Boston Architect Henry Wood, for $3600 in back taxes. Relatives of Mr. Wood still own the property and frequently offer it for weekly rentals on various real estate websites. If you do decide to rent it, remember you must bring in all your supplies, but there is electricity provided by a small windmill and fresh water for showers from a small cistern. If someone needs to send you mail during your stay, the address is 1 Narragansett Bay. And thanks to the 1938 hurricane, the Storm of the Century, you will have to arrive by boat. Enjoy, but keep an eye on the forecast, just in case.

The Roller Coaster at Easton's Beach, destroyed by the Hurricane and never to be rebuilt. (Photo courtesy of the author.)

11

Hurricane Hut

There is a majestic mansion on Ocean Drive, one of the last built at the end of Newport's Gilded Age, that from the outside appears to be idyllic. The outward appearance holds a dark secret, another tragedy from the 1938 Hurricane, "The Storm of the Century."

In 1936, Verner Z. Reed, heir to the Cripple Creek mining fortune and Vice Chairman of the Chase Manhattan bank, chose this 9-acre parcel to build his glamorous summer estate, Seafair. It would be one of the last grand mansions built along Ocean Drive and would signal the tail end of Newport's "Gilded Age." Many locals questioned the location, to build such a grand mansion, literally perched just feet about the unpredictable and at times, unforgiving Atlantic Ocean. Yet Mr. Reed, who later in his life would be Ambassador to Morrocco under President Reagan, pressed ahead with the project, despite warnings from long time local residents. Mr.

Reed was used to getting his way but would soon come up against a formable foe, the undefeated sea, just outside his backdoor.

September 21st, 1938 would be an unforgettable day in the collective psyche for an entire region, for decades to come, but the morning started out like a typical early autumn day. The Reed's were hosting a cocktail hour for some close friends at Seafair, a regular occurrence when they were in town. Guests were enthralled by the unusually high waves, crashing over the seawall, late that fateful afternoon. By 5pm. They started to realize, this wasn't a regular afternoon storm, when seawater began to flood into the first floor. The startled partygoers ascended the spiral staircase to the second floor expecting the upper level to keep them safe from the quickly rising tide. The angry ocean had other ideas, however and continued to rise at an alarming pace. Pieces of the sturdy seawall, built to shield the Mansion from the sea, started to break apart and chunks of the wall could be heard hammering the side of the estate and even the roof. It was becoming crystal clear, the storm surge was rising too fast for the Mansion to withstand and the owners and their guests needed to get out fast, before they drown like rats. The panicked revelers were able to climb through a window at the front of the property, with the sturdy Mansion acting like a shield from the wind whipped waves, down a fire escape, to the front lawn, then up the long driveway, then finally to a neighbor's home just up the hill to higher ground. Everyone thankfully got out alive, before the full force of the 120+ mile per hour winds drove the estimated 15-foot storm surge through Seafair. The Reed's and their guests were lucky. But the shock and awe of the Hurricane kept the owners from returning to their seaside manor for many years.

Less than a decade later, a brush with a massive Hurricane would occur again at Seafair, this time with much more tragic results. With owner, Vernor Z. Reed spending most of his time at his Greenwich, Connecticut enclave, his seaside summer estate, Seafair, was rented out for the summer to some fellow multimillionaires. William Van Alen of Philadelphia would be summering at Seafair, not far from his mother, Daisy Van Alen Bruguiere. Mrs. Van Allen lived at Wakehurst, which is located almost directly across the street from Newport's grandest summer "Cottage" the Breakers. Needless to say, she lived in a very high-end neighborhood.

By September 12, 1944, The United States Weather Bureau was issuing warnings along the Atlantic Seaboard, from Miami to Portland, Maine. The Weather Bureau, who had not yet started naming Hurricanes, dubbed this Category 4, 600-mile-wide monster, "The Great Atlantic Hurricane." Apparently, the Van Alen's were too busy socializing or not overly concerned about the approaching storm, made no pre-hurricane preparations, and carried on without a care in the world. Regrettably, their inaction would prove to be very costly.

On September 15th, 1944, the Great Atlantic Hurricane announced it arrival on the eastern end of Long Island, much like the 1938 storm had 7 years earlier, around 2pm. Less than 2 hours later, a second landfall was recorded at Point Judith, Rhode Island, roughly than 15 miles southwest of Newport. The conditions would go downhill and in a hurry. The Van Alen's loaded their Rolls Royce and tried to make a mad dash up the hill to a neighbor on higher ground at a mansion called Avalon. Tragically, their last minute evacuation was too late. The Rolls Royce was inundated by a wall of water from the Hurricane's storm surge. Mr. Van Alen and his wife Bessie were able to withstand the powerful wave, and eventually found their way to higher ground. The 3 housekeepers, riding in the car with them, were not so lucky. The surge swept them away and their bodies were never found, adding to the storms dreadful total of 28 deaths throughout New England alone. The storm was also responsible for sinking the Navy destroyer USS Warrington, roughly 450 miles east of Vero Beach, Florida, with a loss of an almost unimaginable 248 sailors. Apparently, the term, "The Storm passed safely out to Sea" really doesn't apply, especially to those ships out at sea.

Seafair has been in the news recently but this time for a much more uplifting and positive reason. The seaside manor was recently purchased by comedian and former Tonight Show host Jay Leno for 13.5 million dollars, in 2017. The affable Leno has been a huge positive for the Newport area, with his support of a local theatre called the Firehouse and his efforts to bring Classic Car events to the City by the Sea. It seems the 15,000 square foot mansion commonly known as the "Hurricane Hut" is in good hands for now, although it only has a 6-car garage. Perhaps the noted car collector, with a reported 150 car collection, may need to expand the garage a bit!

Seafair, AKA, The Hurricane Hut, has had a brush with not 1 but 2 killer Hurricanes over its history. (Photo courtesy of the author with an assist from Drone Photos RI.)

12

Chaos at Crossways

If there was one person who was the antithesis of the prim, proper and polite image of the "Gilded Age" and New York and Newport's highest of high society, it was Mamie Fish. While "Mrs. Astor" was considered the Queen of high society, Mrs. Fish was the thorn in her side, or an antagonist who constantly poked holes in the social norms of the day. Mrs. Fish, for lack of a better term, wrote her own rules and didn't seem to care what others thought.

Marion Graves Anthon, came from a fairly well to do family in Staten Island, New York, but her marriage to businessman Stuyvesant Fish in 1876, took her Merry Making to a whole new level. Mr. Fish came from an impressive lineage, his father was Governor and Senator from New York. He also served as Secretary of State for the Grant administration and was a direct descendant of original New Yorker, Peter

Stuyvesant. Mamie, as she was informally known, didn't seem to bother to know too much about her husband's business affairs, she just liked to spend his money. When asked which railroad, he ran, she bluntly replied "One line or the other, frankly they are all the same to me." She was much more concerned about turning High Society upside down and openly mocking its norms, any chance she got!

Mamie would need a Newport summer home as her headquarters to wreak havoc and cause chaos, so Stuyvesant purchased a plot of land across the street from the exclusive Bailey's Beach. Ironically, the ultra-private beach club was the epic center of the highest of high society during the summer season. From her hilltop perch, Mrs. Fish could literally look down on her unsuspecting victims. After 2 years of construction, Mrs. Fish's command center was finally opened for the 1898 summer season. Crossways was a Colonial Revival style property built by famed architect Dudley Newton. Perhaps as a slap in the face to other Newport socialites, Crossways wasn't modeled after a European Palace like most other area summer estates along Bellevue Avenue. Mrs. Fish's seasonal property was modeled after America's most famous home, The White House.

Conceivably, it could have been a coincidence, but most likely it was done intentionally, as a way for Mamie to announce, I am going to entertain in my unique style, High Society be damned!

The Crossways Mansion on Ocean Drive, Mrs. Fish's clubhouse of chaos.

(Photo courtesy of the author.)

Crossways hosted its first official party in July of 1898, as Mrs. Fish flung open the doors at Crossway with a southern themed Barn Dance, certainly nothing that would been seen at most of the other extremely formal Newport Dinner parties. From that day forward, parties and social gatherings at Crossways would devolve into the strange, bizarre as well as outrageous. Mrs. Fish was fond of saying, "Howdy Do. Howdy Do, make yourselves at home! And believe me no one wishes you were there more than me." She introduced the 50 minute dinner party to Newport, where the waitstaff was instructed to literally start clearing the plates, even before guests had finished eating. This was Mamie's response to what she perceived at Mrs. Astor's endlessly boring events, which at times would last hours.

One of her legendary soirées was to honor a Russian Dignitary named Grand Duke Boris and had invited 200 honored guests to celebrate the occasion at Crossways. There was one slight hitch in the plans however, the Grand Duke was double booked at another, more elegant mansion across town. So as dignitaries like New York Senator Chauncey Depew and financier J.P. Morgan looked on, Mrs. Fish announced the cancellation of the guest of honor, but they had someone better! The doors flung open, and there appeared in Royal Robes, carrying a golden scepter, his Imperial Highness, The Czar of Russia. Amazed and awestruck party goers were in shock and started to bow as the foreign dignitary made his way into the ballroom. Then suddenly, a roar of laughter went up amongst the 200 invited party guests, realizing they had momentarily been duped. It wasn't really the Czar of Russia, it was Mamie's Minister of Mischief and right-hand man of shenanigans, Harry Lehr, masquerading as the Czar! From that night on Mrs. Fish's sidekick would be quizzically known as "King Lehr!"

Mrs. Fish and her band of merry makers, including architect Stanford White, Publisher James Gordon Bennet and her minister of mischief, Harry Lehr seated to the left. (Photo acquired in the public domain)

In a never-ending effort to entertain themselves and perhaps out do their neighbors, Mrs. Fish and Harry Lehr seemed to be cooking out something more outlandish every summer. Harry had an idea to invite 100 of Newport's finest pedigreed and pampered pooches to his Bellevue Avenue estate for a dinner party, provided they too were dressed properly for the occasion. Fantasy became reality as 100 dogs arrived, escorted by their owners in their finest formal wear and even little doggie tuxedos. The guests of honor ate a menu of fricasseed bones and pate' served in silver bowls, seated at a smaller table adjacent to their human counterparts. The "Doggie Dinner" as it would come to be known, was so outlandish, it was carried by most major newspapers on their society page.

One summer afternoon, social minister Harry Lehr received a telegram that old friend Joseph Leiter was sailing into Newport the following day and was traveling with a "Corsican Prince." Harry and Mrs. Fish quickly announced to their high society friends they would be hosting Prince Del Drago of Corsica, the following evening at Crossways and only the who's who of Newport would be invited. The evening of the black-tie event, the waitstaff was given strict instructions, not to over serve the prince champagne, because it was reported he was a bit of a light weight and couldn't handle his liquor very well. Joseph Leiter and the guest of honor, Prince Del Drago finally arrived, and the attendees were in stummed silence at what they saw. It turns out Prince Del Drago of Corsica was actually a monkey, dressed in a little prince's costume. Instead of sending the attendees home disappointed, Mrs. Fish decided to have the ball anyway and Prince Del Drago was seated at the head of the table as the guest of honor. After all, what's the worst that could happen?

Mrs. Teresa Fair Olerich, another of Newport's high society hostesses commented, "The monkey was actually better behaved than many other actual princes she had met." That was until the prince, consumed a little bit too much champagne, climbed up into one of the Crossways Chandeliers and started heaving lightbulbs down upon the frightened guests. As you can imagine, there was a mad dash for the exits at that point. However, "The Monkey Ball" as it is now known, was Mrs. Fish's most outlandish and most talked about gathering, even though it really wasn't her intention. The infamous event is still talked about to this day by locals and tour guides alike, when harkening back to the "Gilded Age" and cemented Maime Fish's legacy as part of Newport's colorful 20th century history.

The end of Newport's summer season was always celebrated at Crossway, with one last final and elaborate costume party. In 1913, the theme for the Mother Goose ball was attendees were to dress as their favorite fairy tale characters. Mrs. Fish would preside over her socialite flock, as a fairy queen, because really these people's lives were very much like fairy tales. With their immense wealth, endless celebrations and constant dinner parties, they had very little touch with reality and the struggles of the real world. After that one final grand event, it was a signal for the wealthy out of towners to pack up, return to New York City, and party throughout the winter, until it was time to return to those summer days in Newport.

The Mother Goose Ball was regrettably Mrs. Fish's swan song when it came to merry making. She was in declining health, perhaps from the decades of revelry and nonstop partying, and suffered a cerebral hemorrhage at her Upstate New York Estate in 1915. Marion "Mamie" Fish was only 62 years old.

With the sudden death of Mrs. Fish, the passing of the Income Tax amendment and the drum beat of World War I roared loudly in Europe, the "Gilded Age" and the days of conspicuous consumption, were quickly coming to an end.

   Yes, Mrs. Fish was a real person, as portrayed in the HBO's Gilded Age. She straddled the Old Money New Yorkers like Mrs. Astor but also accepted and entertained the New Money like the Vanderbilts and Berwinds. Her real home is Newport was the Crossways mansion, but for show, Season 1 episode 8, Tucked Up in Newport, the scenes were filmed at the Ledges. The cottage is still owned by the Cushing Family of Boston and is located almost across the street from Crossways.

Mrs. Stuyvesant Fish had her own unique style of entertaining,

And seemed to like to wear bizarre hats, which were popular during the Gilded Age.(Photos acquired in the public domain.)

13

The Poor little rich Girl

You have likely heard the expression, "You can never be too rich or too thin!" Well, that applies to basically everyone, except American Tobacco Company heiress Doris Duke. Ms. Duke, a part time Newport resident with her Bellevue Avenue estate Rough Point, unwitting may have changed the trajectory of her seasonal hometown, with a tragic and "unfortunate accident" in October 1963. Now imagine, at 12 years of age, the only man you will ever truly love, your father, is dead. A man who has warned you "Trust no one!" To confuse matters, your beloved father's death was exacerbated by an evil and wicked mother, which could have easily been the villainess of a Disney Movie. Oh, and by the way, you've inherited your father's fortune of roughly 100 million dollars, in 1925. Without a doubt that's a lot for a pre-teen to digest and comprehend.

James Buchanan Duke and his family lineage was a true rags to riches story. The family farm outside of Durham, North Carolina was essentially destroyed by the Union Army at the end of the civil war in 1865. After rummaging through the ruins of a burned out and collapsed barn, a hand full of tobacco seeds were found. Doris' paternal grandfather, Washington Duke, planted the seeds and was able to cultivate a profitable crop, holding off starvation for another year. The fledgling tobacco farm would eventually evolve into the massive American Tobacco Company, which would eventually control 90% of the U.S. cigarette market. Thanks to a licensing agreement, American Tobacco was the first cigarette manufacturer to use automated rolling machines. They were able to mass produce their "Lucky Strike" brand, leading to a huge contract to supply smokes to the U.S. Military during WWI. James Duke also foresaw the future of power generation in the Carolina's when his hydroelectric powerplants were supplying power to more than 300 cotton mills in the early 1900's. His vision of hydro-electric power generation evolved in the Carolina's power grid, and the regional energy powerhouse, Duke Energy. Even though Mr. Duke had relocated his operations to New York City, he never forgot his Durham, North Carolina roots. He donated 40 million dollars, a substantial sum of money at the time, to a small liberal arts school, then known as Trinity College. To return the favor and honor their benefactor, the school was renamed to honor Mr. Duke's father, Washington and we now know it as one of the finest academic and athletic institutions in the country, Duke University.

Young Doris Duke and her father, James Buchanan Duke, founder of the American Tobacco Company. His advice to his daughter "Trust No One!" (Photo courtesy of the Duke University archives in the public domain.)

In 1935, at the age of 22, Doris would use marriage as an attempt to free herself from her overbearing mother, Nanoline. Doris would marry James Cromwell, a Diplomat and the son of Palm Beach socialite, Eva Stotesbury. Doris' new husband, a democrat, and New Deal politician was more interested in his new wife's deep pockets as well as her political and social connections. The young bride was almost instantly bored from her new husband's lack of attention and his seemingly endless political obligations and was rumored to carry on a number of high-profile affairs during the couple's marriage of convenience. While James Cromwell, was busy trying to climb the political ladder, eventually becoming Ambassador to Canada, and then running a failed Senate campaign, Doris found the arms of many willing partners to keep her occupied. Among the reported lovers were, Actor Errol Flynn, gold medal winning swimmer and Hawaiian surfing legend Duke Kahanamoku and U.S. General George Patton. After a contentious and protracted legal proceeding, James Cromwell and Doris Duke would come to a monetary agreement and finally officially divorce in 1943. During this time, however, there was an event that would traumatize Doris, and eventually come back to haunt her later in life. A daughter named Arden was born prematurely in 1940, but sadly only lived 1 day. James Cromwell was publicly said to be the father, but speculation was the baby was fathered by one of her other lovers, although it was never actually proven. Doctors advised that for medical reasons, Doris Duke shouldn't, have children, but she would be forever tormented after this dreadful and devastating event.

Doris Duke would give marriage another try, but this time for a much more selfish and personal reason, in 1947. Her second and last husband was Porfirio Rubirosa, the jet setting, polo playing Dominican Playboy. Rubi, as he was affectionately called, was once a lieutenant in General Trijillo's Presidential Guard, Ambassador, and most likely a hitman who would eliminate any of his bosses' political enemies if so ordered. Rubirosa's claim to fame was his legendary sexual prowess and according to his string of famous female lovers, he was "extremely physically gifted." Waiters at a famous Paris restaurant, Rubirosa was known to frequent, nicknamed their giant peppermills, "Rubirosas" in homage to their legendary client. Amazingly the nickname stuck, and these large peppermills were known by the same moniker, even in Newport. Doris Duke had a slight problem however, Rubi was actually married to another woman, French actress, Danielle Darrieux. But Doris had learned at a young age, her large fortune was able to buy her whatever she wanted, so a 1 million check was written to Ms. Darrieux for an uncontested divorce. Once again, Doris Duke was able to purchase what she wanted and buy her way out of trouble, a trait that would serve her well, much later in life. Doris and Rubi's marriage was short lived, lasting just over 1 year. Apparently, the gifted Rubirosa had a long line of suitors for his services and apparently was easily distracted by an almost endless stream of beautiful and famous women, even during his marriage to Doris. Porfirio Rubirosa was well compensated in a divorce settlement in 1948, with a $25,000 a year alimony, an African Fishing fleet, several sports cars, a converted B-25 bomber, and a 17th Century Chateau outside of Paris, France. Quite a payday for just over a year of marriage!

Life has a handful of days when you might look back and consider them a life changing event. For Doris Duke, one of those was October 7th, 1966. Ms. Duke and her "Interior Designer", Eduardo Tirella, were heading out of the Rough Point estate, for a meeting with the

Preservation Society around 5 pm. Tirella was helping Doris redecorate her 19th century mansion with some much-needed upgrades. Tirella had been employed for roughly 10 years as the curator of Ms. Duke's expansive art collection, and had some small-time acting roles, but was leaving Doris' employ for a full-time production designer in Hollywood. Doris Duke was not known to handle breakups well, and what transpired next exemplifies that she got her way, one way or the other.

Eduardo was behind the wheel as the rented Dodge Polara station wagon approached the locked rough iron gate of the service entrance, in front of Rough Point. Tirella jumped out to open the heavy gate and Doris slid over into the driver's seat to maneuver the car out of the property. What happened next is still a mystery and open for debate, more than 50 years later. What we do know for sure is the car lurched forward, pinning the terrified Tirella against the gate or under the car. The force of forward momentum from the heavy station wagon pushed the gates open, pinning him under the car and smashing violently into a tree directly across the street. When the police arrived, they didn't even realize there was a second person involved in the 1 car crash, until Doris Duke inconsolably cried out, "Where is Eduardo? Where is he? "Upon further inspection, curiously, the officer found no blood on the gate nor on the bumper of the crumpled car, contradicting what Doris Duke would later report. Under the vehicle, they did find some brain matter, skin and an eyeball but couldn't locate a body of a victim. They concluded, as a result of being dragged under the car, across the street and eventually smashing into a sturdy tree, the brute force seemed to have ground poor Eduardo Tirella to pieces.

An unhinged Doris Duke was so inconsolable, she would spend the night at Newport Hospital, heavily sedated. It wasn't until the next day that Ms. Duke had calmed down sufficiently and was able to try to piece together what occurred the previous afternoon. Despite eyewitness accounts that the duo had been seen in heated exchanges while antique shopping, Doris contradicted those accounts to investigators. The staff at Rough Point also heard yelling between the pair when Eduardo informed Doris, he was leaving her employ and returning to Hollywood. Doris vehemently denied those claims and insisted they were on amicable terms. From what little she could recall, she was confused over the push button shifter on the rented Dodge station wagon and for some unexplained reason, the vehicle lurched forward, pinning her helpless victim. She claimed after releasing the parking brake, she confused the gas and brake pedals causing a rapid and uncontrollable acceleration. Before the panicked driver could react, the next thing she knew, the car was a steaming, crumpled heap, stopped by the tree across the street from the wrought iron gates. It was all just a blur, she recalled.

After a short investigation, Chief Radice announced the death of Eduardo Tirella was the result of "an unfortunate accident" and no charges would be filed against Doris Duke. Did the tobacco heiress get away with murder? Did she kill her long-time companion and possible lover in a fit of jealous rage? Did her deep pockets get her out of trouble, cementing in her mind, she was above the law? Well, there are many factors that point to yes about all those still unsolved questions.

Doris Duke did pay a small settlement in a civil lawsuit filed in a wrongful death case by Tirella's family. Chief Radice did retire suddenly, just 5 months after the incident and short investigation. The former chief had retired to Hollywood, Florida, purchased a couple of high-end condos and reportedly had a large sum of money deposited into a bank account from an unnamed source. For the rest of his life, the former Newport police chief denied he received any payments from the tobacco heiress. Another interesting aspect of the case was Doris, who was notoriously tight fisted with charitable donations miraculously found a giving side! She almost immediately donated $25,000 to restore the parts of the damaged Cliff walk, which ran behind her Newport Mansion, Rough Point. Even more miraculously Ms. Duke founded the Newport Restoration Foundation, whose mission is to preserve and protect Colonial Homes that had fallen into disrepair, in the city's Historic Downtown. Close friends of Ms. Duke frequently commented, she deplored seeing those rundown properties on the way to her Bellevue Avenue Estate. Was this a way for Doris to say Thank You to Newport for not looking too deeply into this little mess? Once again, the signs point to yes. The Newport Restoration Foundation does currently have more than 80 historic structures, most from the 18th century, in its portfolio, and many are rented out to local residents. Perhaps the Foundation is the one silver lining from the dark cloud that still hovers over that fateful day, October 7th, 1966.

The crumpled Dodge station wagon, across the street from the Rough Point Mansion, tragically killing Eduardo Tirella. Was it really an "unfortunate accident?" (Photo courtesy of the A.P.I.)

Amazing, this seemingly never-ending mystery took another bizarre turn in 2021, when a then 13-year-old paper boy, claims her heard and saw the incident, while delivering the Newport Daily News. He claims he heard 2 people arguing rather loudly behind the locked gates. As he approached on his bicycle, he heard the

Dodge Polara's V-8 engine rev, then a car crash through the gate and the screams of a man, yelling nooooo! He then claims the revving engine paused for a moment, then the tires squealed, more horrified screams and a secondary crash, into the tree across the street. When the young man finally arrived at the scene, a tall regal woman, stepped out of the car. The startled paper boy asked, "Can I help you Ma'am?" The frazzled woman abruptly turned to the frighted bystander, shook her bony finger at him and warned... "You better get the hell out of here!" So, he did, pedaling his bike away, returning home to tell his father what he had just seen. His father knew what type of woman Doris Duke was and warned his young son to keep his mouth shut. She was rich and powerful enough that if she wanted to, she could have one of her henchmen run him over with a truck on his paper route, and call that an accident as well. The secret was kept all these decades, but with all the key players long since dead, the now 60+ year old felt the truth should come out. Crime scene investigators, with the new evidence concluded, Tirella was most likely alive when the car careened through the gate, jumping onto the hood for safety and peering shockingly through the windshield. Doris then hit the brakes, flinging her victim under the car, then accelerated again, to crush him under the heavy rear axle. This would explain the lack of blood on the inside of the gate and the hood. The Newport Police briefly reopened the case based on the new evidence presented, but quicky came to the same conclusion, Eduardo Tirella died from an "unfortunate accident." Doris Duke's influence still resonated, even from beyond the grave!

Over the years, Doris Duke's growing catalog of scandals and controversies continued to grow, as did her vast fortune. It was estimated that she earned a cool million dollars a week, just in dividends from Duke Power, the stock she inherited from her father's energy company. For a woman whose mantra, was trust no one, she was duped later in life, by someone who pulled on her hard-to-reach heart strings. But Chandi Hefner was able to pull it off, receiving a massive payday in the process. In 1985, Doris was introduced to Chandi, a Hari Krishna devotee in Hawaii, and quickly became part of Doris' inner circle. Chandi had enough intimate knowledge of Doris' inner pain over the loss of her only child Arden, 45 years earlier, to get inside her head and steal her heart. Chandi was able to convince her unwitting target, that she was the reincarnation of Arden, and divine fate had brought them together at last. The usually hesitant and suspicious Doris Duke was overjoyed and quicky legally adopted the con artist as her long-lost daughter, despite the objections of her counsel. By 1991, Doris was growing suspicious of her adopted daughter, and was increasingly becoming more paranoid. She confided to others in her increasingly shrinking inner circle, she thought Chandi was trying to poison her. Doris finally realized she had been conned but at this point it was too late. By legally adopting Chandi, the grifter was entitled to an iron clad trust fund, set up for any child of Doris', natural or adopted, by her father James Buchanan Duke. Chandi would eventually collect a 65 million dollars settlement to forego any future claims to the vast Duke inheritance and was able to keep the pineapple plantation Doris purchased for her in Hawaii.

As bizarre and almost unbelievable as the Heffner situation was, Doris had an even more outrageous scandal that would close out her life and would carry on for years, even after her death. Around the time the newly adopted daughter came into her life, a new head butler was hired to oversee the household staff, on the recommendation of all people, singer Peggy Lee.

His name was Bernard Lafferty. He moved to the United States at a young age after being orphaned in Ireland, eventually finding work as the maître d' in the Versailles Room of the posh Beverly-Stratford Hotel in Philadelphia. This is where the redheaded, ponytailed, often drunk and barefoot butler met any of the famous people he would eventually work for. After freezing Chandi out of her life, Doris and Bernard retreated to her Beverly Hills Mansion called Falcon Lair, originally built for silent film star, Rudolph Valentino. Doris, now in failing health, was becoming much more dependent on Bernard, and he kept her increasingly isolated from the world. By 1992, Doris was contemplating another face lift in her never-ending attempt to remain young, and her butler was encouraging her to have it. Just 2 days after the procedure she fell and broke her hip, essentially rendering her a prisoner in her Beverly Hills Estate. Bernard was in total control of her business and personal life. Anyone who would dial Falcon Lair to check on her condition, Bernard would reply in his amicable Irish accent, "Ms. Duke is fine; however, she can't come to the phone right now. I will tell her you called." Of course, he never relayed any messages. In 1993, the now

80-year-old heiress wanted to have her ailing knees replaced and of course her loyal butler was all for it. The especially painful surgeries left her almost 100% disabled and had to use a wheelchair when she wasn't bed ridden. Bernard took full advantage of the situation, while Doris lay in a semi-comatose, pain killer induced state of consciousness, Bernard was getting chauffeured to the bars, nightclubs, and discos of West Hollywood. Other days, the Rolls Royce would cruise to Rodeo Drive for extravagant shopping sprees. All of course on her dime, because at this point, he controlled her seemingly endless purse strings.

Finally on October 28th, 1993, Doris Duke passed at her Beverly Hills mansion, perhaps of natural causes or perhaps with a lethal injection of Demerol and Morphine. There were strict instructions in her will that her body was to be thrown into the Pacific Ocean and eaten by sharks, a ritual she had learned about during her time in Hawaii. Her last will and testament also stated her eyes were to be bequeathed to the New York Eye Clinic as an organ donation, but this wish was never carried out either. Bernard quickly had Doris' body cremated and tossed her ashes over the Pacific Ocean. This hasty decision ended any opportunity for a medical examiner to perform an autopsy to determine the actual cause of death. It's as if someone wanted to dispose of the corpse swiftly, hide any evidence of foul play and ensure the person named executor and benefactor of such a large estate would receive their enormous windfall. But who would have prior knowledge of where the vast sums of money would be distributed after her passing? Well of course, the only person who was by her side, offering advice, while she was kept isolated from the entire world, the Irish Butler, Bernard Lafferty.

Shockingly, the often drunk, barefoot, and illiterate butler, was named executor of the vast fortune, valued at 1.3 billion dollars, and would receive a $500,000 annual salary to oversee the distribution of funds to Ms. Duke's multiple charities named in her will.

Bernard Lafferty purchased his own 2.5-million-dollar Bel Air mansion, dyed his hair blond, cut his signature ponytail, and lost a considerable amount of weight. He also began wearing his former boss's clothes and jewelry, parading himself around Hollywood and other Los Angeles hot spots, for all to see, the person in charge of the Doris Duke Charities. It almost as if the former butler was trying to transform himself into a living incarnation of his former boss. Certainly, bizarre behavior to say the least. Lafferty's lavish lifestyle of illicit drugs, expensive brandy and designer clothes caught the attention of the Law Firm overseeing the assets, intended to go to charity according to the strict instructions outlined in the will. It seems the extensive bar tabs and clothing receipts were being charged to the charities as expenses. A judge intervened and Bernard Lafferty was ousted as head of the Duke Charites, turning over the duties to a board of directors instead, who would finally carry out Ms. Duke's last will and testament as she painstakingly laid out. Not surprisingly, almost 3 years to the day of Doris Duke's mysterious passing, Bernard Lafferty was found dead of an apparent heart attack, at the age of 51.

The roughly 1.2 billion dollars remaining in Doris Duke's estate would remain in trusts to support causes she supported throughout her life. These included various art programs, prevention of cruelty to animals and the Newport Restoration Foundation, which now operates her Newport Mansion Rough Point as a museum. Doris Duke was a complicated and controversial person to say the least. As far as

Newport, Rhode Island is concerned, her preservation effort has had a lasting impact on maintaining the charm of the colonial district. It was also her vision to construct the hugely popular Queen Anne's Square just below Trinity Church. For these efforts, all of us who adore Newport and its colonial history will be eternally grateful, albeit at a huge cost, the loss of a human life on Bellevue Avenue.

Doris and the executor of her will and former butler, Bernard Lafferty, the last person to see the tobacco heiress alive.

(Photo courtesy of US Weekly.)

14

Reversal of Fortune

A quick drive up and down Newport's exclusive thoroughfare, Bellevue Avenue, reveals an almost unbelievable collection of replicas of European Palaces and Mansions. Incredibly, many of these breathtakingly exquisite properties hold secrets and scandals behind their golden gilded gates, and immaculately manicures hedges. Clarendon Court is one such place, where a still unsolved incident took place just before Christmas 1980 and kicked off what was one known as "The Trial of the Century."

A quick glimpse of Martha "Sunny" Crawford von Bulow's life would suggest she had a fairy tale existence. She was the heiress to a 75-million-dollar fortune, thanks to her father's gas and electric company. She was a classic beauty, often favorably compared to a young Grace Kelly, had 3 beautiful, bright children, and was once married to an Austrian Prince. She seemed happily married to a Danish born attorney, Claus von Bulow and had homes in both New York City and Newport, Rhode Island, with a staff of attentive servants to wait on her every whim. From outward appearances, Sonny's life was a dream, but in reality, she wasn't happy.

The couple was frequently at each other's throats, arguing over money and Claus' desire to return to work. He was once a high-profile attorney, and personal assistant, for the eccentric billionaire J. Paul Getty, and was tired of living off his wife's monthly allowance. Another bone of contention was the open marriage arrangement the couple had agreed upon. Apparently, Claus was permitted to fool around with anyone he chose, as long as the person was not part of the moneyed couples society circle. Claus openly broke their agreement, when he started publicly dating Alexandra Isles, an actress in the popular sci-fi soap opera, Dark Shadows.

The event that took place on December 21st, 1980 at Sunny's seaside Mansion Clarendon Court, would thrust the seaside resort in the national media's spotlight, for years to come. That evening Sunny was rather incoherent and badly slurring her speech. Her son, Alexander also noticed Sunny was struggling to walk and had difficulty getting into bed. The concerned son summoned Claus from his study, where he was going over paperwork, to aid Sunny and put her to bed. Alexander was concerned, and rightfully so, Sunny was trying to overdose on sleeping pills, but a seemingly unconcerned Claus dismissed the claim. He insisted Sunny was just overtired and stressed about the upcoming holidays and would be fine after a good night of sleep.

Around 11am, the family gathered around the breakfast table, but Sunny was nowhere to be found. She was a notoriously late sleeper, so no one was seriously concerned at this point. Claus arrived a short time later and inquired to his wife's whereabouts. No one in the household had seen her that morning, so an alarmed Claus quickly realized he better check on her! When Claus burst into his wife's ample bathroom, he was reportedly aghast at what he found. Sunny was sprawled out, unconscious on the tile floor, bleeding from her lip. Her nightgown was bunched around her waist, and she was laying lifelessly in a pool of her own urine. Most alarmingly, her rigid body was ice cold! An ambulance was summoned, and the unresponsive heiress was quickly transported to Newport Hospital where her body temperate was reported to be an almost unbelievable 81 degrees. Sunny was still alive but barely and would be transported to a Boston Trauma center, for more cutting-edge care in an attempt to save her swiftly fading life. The trauma center administered a CAT scan which revealed a dire diagnosis, Sunny was in a coma which was irreversible.

This is when the whispers and allegations began to fly, especially from Sunny's 2 children from her earlier marriage to the Austrian Prince, Ala and Alexander. They were convinced beyond a shadow of a doubt, Claus had murdered their mother, to collect his share of the inheritance. They certainly had enough evidence to be suspicious with Claus' indifference to her coma and his insistence she be removed from life support systems. It was no secret that Claus' new mistress, Alexandra Isles had expensive tastes and a reported 15 million dollar cut from the will, would sure go a long way to keep her happy.

Apparently, the rumors, allegations and circumstantial evidence were enough for a grand jury to investigate, eventually indicting Claus von Bulow, for attempted murder. The trial of the century and the media circus that follows were about to descend on Newport, whether they were ready or not.

Claus von Bulow leaving the side entrance of the Newport County Court House.

(Photo courtesy of WCBT TV.)

With the initial arraignment of von Bulow, on July 31st, 1981, literally every news station and media outlet, including the major networks, had crews and reporters camped out in the square below the Newport County Court house. This was just a foreshadowing of what was to come. The trial, at least for this century, would commence in February 1982 with the nightly news programs leading their evening broadcasts with highlights and testimony from the sensationalized, attempted murder trial taking place in Newport. For the next month a parade of witness', family friends, doctors and medical experts would testify, thrusting Newport into the national spotlight in newspaper headlines, gossip magazines and Television broadcasts. Von Bulow's defense team tried to paint his wife as depressed, suicidal and had attempted to take her life in the past. The prosecution exposed Von Bulow as a womanizer, philanderer and self-serving husband who cared little for his wife, except to inherit a portion of her sizable fortune. They also focused on a black bag which was found by a private investigator, hired by the family. The black bag contained insulin and needles, was subsequently turned over to the police as evidence. Prosecutors argued the insulin was

Claus' murder weapon of choice, injecting his wife, who was hypo-glycemic, with the potentially lethal shots, inducing her into an irreversible coma. The jury agreed with the prosecution and on March 16, 1982, Claus von Bulow was convicted on 2 counts of attempted murder earning him a prison sentence of 30 years behind bars.

While out on bail, awaiting appeal of his conviction, Claus was putting together his own legal dream team, in hopes he would never spend a day in jail. He convinced noted Harvard Law professor Alan Dershowitz to handle his appeal, with a new trial, in front of the Rhode Island Supreme Court. Dershowitz put together a team of Harvard law students to scrutinize the evidence and look for new clues to ensure their new client was found not guilty by any means necessary. The team of bright, up and coming legal minds included future CNBC stock market prognosticator Jim Cramer, and one day New York Attorney General and Governor, Eliot Spitzer.

The bright, young legal eagles scoured all the evidence presented at the previous trial and came up with an overlooked legal nugget. If this evidence could be called into question during the appeal, potentially it could be Claus' get out of jail free card. It turns out, the black bag containing insulin, the syringes and other pills was found by a private detective, then handed off to the police as evidence. Medical Experts also testified that insulin could not have caused such a powerful and irreversible coma. Only the self-ingestion of pills mixed with alcohol could lead to such a devastating result. Attorney Alan Dershowitz was a master of casting doubt on evidence gathering, pounding the table that the evidence was planted in an effort to frame his client. This was a tactic Dershowitz would use throughout his legal career, especially during the next trial of the century, when he was part of the O.J. Simpson legal "Dream Team" less than a decade later. Due to the possibility the evidence was planted combined with Sunny's self-destructive lifestyle that was exposed in court, the jurists had no other choice. On June 10th, 1985, Claus Von Bulow walked out of Rhode Island Supreme Court a free man, acquitted of all charges.

There were still some legal wranglings, even after the acquittal, mostly over the reported 100-million-dollar inheritance. Sunny's first 2 children from her previous marriage, were still convinced Claus had killed their mother, so a legal agreement was drafted where von Bulow would divorce Sunny, then agree to renounce any and all claims to the Crawford Family fortune. Part of the compromise they agreed upon was Claus and Sunny's daughter, Cosimo, would be reinstated and was legally entitled to her share of the enormous estate.

Claus never felt comfortable again, living in the States, especially with the whispers and innuendo he had gotten away with murder. Whether or not he committed the crime, he was shunned by most of the social circles and acquaintances he enjoyed while married to Sunny. Claus von Bulow would eventually settle in London, finding a new career as a Theatre critic. He would pass away peacefully at his London home, May 25,2019, at the age of 92.

Sunny would never regain consciousness and lived in a vegetative state at a private nursing facility, in New York City. She would still have her hair and nails done on a regular basis and would occasionally curl her lips into a wry smile or slightly open an eye. Sadly, when her children would visit and spend time with her, occasionally a lone tear would run down her face. Perhaps their voices brought back a memory deep in her unconscious state or was just sad she was no longer able to communicate with them. After nearly 28 years in her irreversible coma, Sunny finally passed away on December 6th, 2008. Sunny would be laid to rest, not far from where the tragic incident occurred, at Saint Mary's Episcopal cemetery in Portsmouth, Rhode Island. On her tombstone is inscribed Martha Sharp Crawford…Sunny.

Alan Dershowitz wrote a book about his experiences during the von Bulow trial, and it was made into a movie called "Reversal of Fortune." The movie gave some really interesting insight as to what kind of person Claus von Bulow really was. Jeremy Irons won the 1991 Academy Award for his portrayal of the convicted, then acquitted murderer, with Glen Close playing the troubled Sunny. Irons was able to capture the complexity of the main character who could be charming, cynical, conniving, sinister with an air of mystery and aloofness, almost all at the same time. During one scene when Dershowitz and von Bulow are lunching at Delmonico's, before the lawyer has even agreed to take the case, the waiter drops off their food, and addresses them as Professor Dershowitz, Dr von Bulow.

"When I was married to Sunny, we never got this table. Now, two injections of insulin and I'm a doctor."

Another line from the film that stood out and that seemed to encapsulate the darkness he kept inside, was after a stroll the 2 characters had, while discussing the intricate details of the case. Dershowitz wants the truth, man to man, of the events the evening before and then the following morning when Sunny was found unconscious on her bathroom floor. The almost astonished and perplexed Dershowitz character, played masterfully by Ron Silver, when hearing von Bulow's opaque and tacit responses, remarks to Claus:

"You are a very strange man."

Jeremy Irons as Von Bulow responds in a semi-British, Aristocratic accent and wry smile "You have no Idea!" as he climbs into the back seat of his chauffeured limousine…

15

Titanic Decisions

George Dunton Widner had a very good life. He had inherited a profitable business from his father, the Philadelphia Traction Company, which operated cable and electric streetcars in the city of Brotherly Love. He was in the process of building his dream summer "Cottage" on an 8-acre parcel of land overlooking the Atlantic Ocean along Newport, Rhode Island's millionaires' row, Bellevue Avenue. During the spring of 1912, he, and his family, would steam off to Paris, France to interview a French Chef for his Ritz Carlton Hotel, in Philadelphia. His wife Elanor, and son Harry, a Harvard Grad, were along for this wonderful journey…How could life get any better?

It is truly amazing how someone's life can change on a dime, but in the Widener's case, it came down to one decision, altering the family legacy forever. Mrs. Widner had a wonderful idea, as a way to finish off the trip to Europe and make it truly memorable. The family would book passage back to America on the new White Star Lines luxury ocean liner, the R.M.S. Titanic, sailing from Southampton, England on April 10th, 1912. (R.M.S. signified Royal Mail Ship, so besides passengers the vessel also carried mail and freight.)

The ship's first-class registry read like the who's who of the business world, politics, and high society. Included on the passenger list were White Star's chairman J. Bruce Ismay, American Industrialist Benjamin Guggenheim, Macy's Department Store owner Isadore Strauss, Canadian Brewing tycoon Harry Molson and a Denver socialite named Molly Brown, just to name a few. Titanic would dock the next day in Cherbourg, France to onboard some more First-class passengers including another part-time Newport resident, Colonel John Jacob Astor IV and his new wife, Madeline. Astor was most likely the wealthiest of all the Titanic's passengers. Ironically Banker J.P. Morgan, chocolatier Milton Hershey and railroad heir Alfered Gwynne Vanderbilt had all booked passage for this maiden voyage as well, but fate intervened, and plans were changed at the last moment. Once again, one decision can have life altering effects! After 1 final stop in Ireland to pick up mail and 3rd class passengers, Titanic was finally on its way to New York City, with a scheduled arrival of April 17th, 1912. Veteran White Star Line Captain, Edward John Smith was at the helm at a healthy 22 knot clip. This would be considered a rather dangerous speed, especially with the iceberg warnings in the chilly North Atlantic waters. It was likely White Star's chairman, J. Bruce Ismay was pressuring Captain Smith to steam at the high rate of speed to set a record for the Titanic's maiden voyage. Any record for a Trans- Atlantic crossing would generate a massive amount of positive and free publicity in both domestic and international newspapers. Once again, another decision that would have monumental and life altering consequences…

The Titanic's voyage did not get off to a splendid start, however, perhaps a foreshadowing of events to come? Upon the initial departure from Southampton, England the massive ocean liner caused such a huge wake in the harbor, it snapped the mooring lines of 2 other liners, causing them to drift aimlessly. Only the quick actions of Captain Smith, who ordered the powerful engines to full astern and the nimble maneuverings of a nearby tugboat, prevented the S.S. City of New York, from crashing full force into the starboard side of Titanic. Witnesses claimed there was barely 4 feet between the 2 liners and a catastrophic collision. Even more amazingly, there was a fire raging in one of Titanic's coal bunkers approximately 10 days prior to the ship's departure and continued to burn for several days into its voyage. Not surprisingly, passengers were kept unaware of this situation. Fires occurred frequently in the bunkers deep below steamships at the time, due to spontaneous combustion of the coal and its dust. The fires had to be extinguished with fire hoses by moving the coal on top to another bunker and then removing the burning coal and feeding it into the furnace. The fire was finally extinguished on April 14th, 5 days into Titanic's maiden voyage. There has also been some speculation that the fire and attempts to extinguish it may have made the ship more vulnerable to its eventual demise, with the intense heat weakening the exterior steel plates.

Also contributing to the perils, the Titanic's faced on its west bound journey, was the persistent warnings of icebergs on its route to pier 59 on New York City's west side. Yet, veteran Captain Smith seemed unconcerned, with numerous trans-Atlantic crossings under his belt, he had navigated these North Atlantic waters dozens of times. Conventional maritime thinking of the time was icebergs posed little threat to Ocean going vessels of the day. In 1907 a German liner, S.S. Krownprinz Wilhelm, hit an iceberg head on and was able to complete its voyage. Even Captain Smith weighed in on the likelihood of a catastrophe resulting in a collision with one of these massive blocks of ice. Captain Smith himself had declared in 1907 that he "could not imagine any condition which would cause a ship to founder. Modern shipbuilding has gone beyond that." After all, Titanic was the largest ship ever to sail and had every modern technological advance, including watertight compartments, and sealable bulkheads, making it "Virtually Unsinkable."

The R.M.S. Titanic departing Southampton, England, September 10th, 1912. More than 1500 passengers would never reach their final destination, including Mr. Widner and his son, Harry.

(Photo courtesy of the Titanic research association.)

The evening of April 14th, 1912, started out rather routinely aboard Titanic, although the captain did alter the ship's course to a bit more southerly track, but did not reduce speed. At 10pm there was a shift change and 2 well rested crew members climbed into the crow's nest for that evening's lookout duty. The night was unusually calm, making icebergs more difficult to see, because there were no waves breaking around the base of the massive ice flows. Not helping the lookouts was the fact that the crow's nest's binoculars had been misplaced. At 10:55pm. a nearby ship, The S.S. Californian, radioed the Titanic: "Say, old man, we are stopped and surrounded by ice." The annoyed telegraph operator responded angrily: "Shut up! Shut up! I am busy. I am working Cape Race." (A wireless telegraph station was located at Cape Race, Newfoundland, Canada.) He was busy trying to send passenger's messages and correspondence to shore and never relayed the warning to the Titanic's bridge. At 11:35 pm. a lookout spots an iceberg dead ahead and rings the bell three times to indicate that something is in their path. He then calls the bridge and 2nd Officer Murdoch, in command on the bridge, orders the Titanic "hard-a-starboard" (to the left) and the engines reversed. He also ordered the doors to the supposedly watertight compartments closed. Tragically it is too late, at 11:40 PM, The starboard side of the Titanic scrapes along the vast, mostly submerged, iceberg. Shortly thereafter, Captain Smith arrives on deck and is told the sobering news, the ship has struck an iceberg, and the mail room is filling with water. Other reports soon come in of water in at least five of the ship's compartments. The Titanic's Designer Thomas Andrews, along for the maiden voyage, surveys the damage. The "Virtually Unsinkable" liner was built to remain afloat with only four compartments flooded, not 5 or more. Andrews makes the dire prediction, that the ship has only about one to two hours before sinking.

At Midnight, April 15, 1912, Captain Smith gave the order he never could have dreamed of, Launch the Lifeboats, women, and children first. Multiple distress signals are sent from the wireless room and emergency distress flares and rockets were launched, but the closest ship that responded to the S.O.S, the Carpathia, is more than 3 hours away. There were reports of a mystery ship, spotted from the Titanic, within visual range. It was later determined that it was a Norwegian Flagged vessel illegally hunting seals in the ice flow and did not respond to the distress signals to avoid being caught. Another ship in the general vicinity, The S.S. Californian, which had radioed an earlier ice warning, switched off its radio for the evening with the operator turning in for the night, and tragically, did not respond to the distress rockets.

Many of the lifeboats were launched half-full, due to the passenger's unshakable belief they were safer on Titanic, due to its invincibility, than in a wooden rowboat on the icy North Atlantic. But by 2 am. it was becoming clear; the ship doesn't have much time left afloat. The Titanic's bow, rapidly filling with seawater, had sunk low enough that the stern's massive propellers are now clearly visible above the waterline. At 2:18 am, the lights finally went out, plunging the ship into darkness. As the massive ocean liner slips beneath the waves, almost vertical at this point, the air inside causes a massive internal explosion from the pressure. The ship literally cracks in half, between the 3rd and 4th funnels and by 2:20am, the stern has disappeared below the sea, leaving hundreds of survivors struggling in the icy waters. The Titanic is gone.

The lifeboats that had space, rowed back toward the wreckage field, trying to pluck survivors out of the frigid sea. With water temperatures estimated to be around 28 degrees, the human body can only withstand a few minutes of exposure, before hypothermia sets in. Of the hundreds of passengers who survived the initial sinking, only 10 souls who were pulled from the freezing North Atlantic would live.

At 4:10 am, the R.M.S. Carpathia, who had heeded the distress call, was the first ship to arrive and began to gather the survivors out of the lifeboats. At 5:30 am. the controversial vessel S.S. Californian switched on their wireless receiver and got the grim news; Titanic had sunk overnight. The merchant vessel finally arrived on the scene around 8:30 am, passing the departing Carpathia, which had already picked up all remaining survivors and was steaming toward New York City. The Californian searched the wreckage field for a couple hours, but it was a fruitless endeavor. They only found scattered wreckage, empty lifeboats, and sadly, lifeless corpses floating in their life belts.

On April 18, around 9:15pm. The Carpathia finally arrived at the Cunard Lines Pier 54 on

New York City's West Side. This is when the true magnitude of the tragedy was finally realized. Of the 2220 passengers and crew that departed from Europe only 705 eventually arrived in New York. The icy North Atlantic Claimed the rest, 832 passengers and 685 crew, roughly 350 miles of the coast of Newfoundland, Canada.

Among the extensive casualty list was part time Newporter, and wealthiest passenger on board, John Jacob Astor IV. He was identified by his embroidered initials sewn on the label of his jacket and the gold pocket watch he always kept with him. His new wife Madeline Force and her maid were placed on one of the lifeboats and would survive the sinking. Astor's recovered body was buried in The Trinity Church Cemetery in Manhattan.

Captain Edward Smith was last seen on the bridge, just about the same time as the huge smokestacks collapsed. The captain apparently went down with his ship, but his body was never recovered.

Our man who had it all, George Widner and his 27-year-old son Harry, also perished during the sinking, however Eleanor Widner and her maid, did survive. Mrs. Widner would oversee the final construction of her 30,000 square foot Seaside Estate, Miramar, hosting an opening night gala in August of 1915. Mrs. Widener wanted a lasting tribute to her son, Harry, a Harvard Graduate. She commissioned Horace Trumbauer, the same architect who designed Miramar, to create a library on the Harvard campus as a lasting memory of her son. At a cost of more than 3 million dollars and containing upwards of 3.5 million books, the Harry Elkins Widner Memorial Library proudly stands on the Harvard Campus. There was even a rumor that Mrs. Widner attached a stipulation to Harvard University in order to receive this generous gift. She wanted all graduating Harvard students to be able to pass a swim test, although it is unlikely swimming proficiency could have saved her son in the chilly waters that fateful morning. A noble thought none the less…

The Widner's seaside summer home, Miramar is still in big demand, this time to a new generation of high-powered businesspeople and financiers. Blackstone Asset Management Chairman and CEO Stephen Schwarzman purchased the seaside villa for a reported 27 million dollars in 2021. Before we start a go fund me page to help Mr. Schwartzman to help cover the upkeep of Miramar, his reported net worth is estimated to be over 50 billion dollars. Welcome to Billionaires Row, Bellevue Avenue, Mr. Schwarzman.

Two of Newport's wealthiest summer residents perished during the sinking of the R.M.S. Titanic, George Widner and John Jacob Astor IV.

(Image acquired in the public domain.)

16

Alva

There are a handful of people and celebrities who can just be identified by only a one-word title. Madonna, Prince, Chong, Liberace and even Oprah. Newport had their own version for a one name moniker. Her name was Alva, and her influence still resonates in Newport to this day.

Alva Erskine Smith was born in Mobile, Alabama to a wealthy shipping merchant who relocated his family to New York City during the civil war. Alva would attend the finest girl's schools in Paris, where she learned to speak French fluently. This is where Alva observed pomp and circumstance at many of the palaces throughout Europe. The style of entertaining she observed with its proper etiquette would influence her later in life. Her early years in France would also influence greatly the style of architecture she preferred, and when she had her massive bankroll, would replicate those European palaces, in multiple locations.

Alva had her sights set on gaining her place in high society and would achieve this goal by almost any means possible. She was tenacious, pugnacious, and not a person who took no for an answer very well. Although her family was fairly well to do, her ultimate social and financial goals would require someone with an almost unlimited bank account.

In the summer of 1874, Alva would find such a man, on a trip to White Sulphur Spring, West Virginia. The area was known for its lavish resorts where wealthy single bachelors would vacation and network with other business magnates of the day. Alva struck gold, marrying New York Central railroad heir, William K Vanderbilt, whose grandfather the Commodore, had amassed an almost unfathomable 100-million-dollar fortune. The couple's wedding in April of 1875 was the most lavish New York City had ever witnessed and was considered the social event of the year. Alva would share with close friends her mantra, "First marry for money, then marry for love." Alva's next step would be to get her "New Money" Vanderbilt's in the ranks of New York's high society, but she needed the approval of 1 person. The Mrs. Astor was the gatekeeper of the exclusive "400" and was no easy task to gain her approval. But Alva was cunning and devised a plan that even Mrs. Astor would sit up and take notice.

Alva's first step to announce her and her family's arrival, was to build replicas of the French Palaces she had seen as a young girl, here in America. To accomplish her feat, the services of Americas preeminent architect were procured, and together, they would change the landscape of New York's 5th Avenue and later, Newport. The architect she chose for this monumental task was Richard Morris Hunt, the first American to ever train at the prestigious Ecole de Beau Arts, in Paris. With Hunt's training and Alva's deep pockets, this unlikely duo would create design and construction magic. The finished masterpiece was the Petit Chateau, a blending of late French Gothic style and Beaux-Arts refinement for the design of the three-and-a-half-story mansion. 660 Fifth Avenue was so grand, it took up an entire city block.

To christen the new home, Alva announced to everyone who was anyone in New York social circles, she was hosting a costume ball of 1200 invitees to show off her massive new chateau. In early 1883, invitations started to trickle out, and the buzz about the event was starting to grow. Even Carrie Astor, the youngest daughter of New York's high society custodian, Caroline Astor, was eagerly preparing for the big event. All of Carrie's friends had already received their golden tickets, and the young ladies had started choreographing their dance routines called quadrilles. Oddly, a week before the big night, Carrie's invite still hadn't arrived. When some mutual friends inquired why the young Miss Astor had been snubbed to that point, part 2 of Alva's master plan was revealed. Since Mrs. Astor never called on Alva for an official introduction, they had never been properly introduced and that violated polite social protocol of the day. Without an official introduction, Carrie would be excluded from the grandest ball of the calendar year. Mrs. Astor knew she had been outflanked by a formable and conniving foe and summoned her carriage, for the short ride up 5th Avenue. Mrs. Astor, basically hat in hand, arrived at 660 5th Avenue, and dropped off her gold embossed calling card, The Mrs. Astor. Alva knew what this gesture meant, she had finally kicked down the door to enter high society, with her inclusion into the "400." There was no coincidence that Carrie and Mrs. Astor's handwritten invitations arrived the following day.

On March 28, 1883, the evening of the gala had finally arrived, and guests were arriving in their elaborate costumes to cheers of bystanders who had gathered along 5th Avenue of course interspersed with the paparazzi. The reported cost of the costume ball was $250,000, a small price to pay for Alva to show that she had arrived. The hostess was decked out as a venetian noblewoman but was upstaged by her normally reserved sister-in-law. Alice Vanderbilt, the wife of New York Central Railroad chairman Cornelius Vanderbilt II, arrived bedazzles in jewels, dressed as an invention, the electric light. Another pressure packed moment was the arrival of society scion, Mrs. Astor. As she was quizzed by the press on her way inside, she conceded to her new money adversary, "We have no right to exclude those whom this great country has brought forward, the time has come for the Vanderbilts." All of the 1200 guests in attendance were required to come in costume except two, Vanderbilt family patriarch, William Henry and former U.S. president, Uyless S. Grant. By all accounts, the evening long festival, which stretched into the early morning hours of the next day, was a smashing success. Alva had pulled off the almost impossible, so onto the next step in the plan, for total domination!

Now that the New York City mansion had been completed, Alva turned her attention to the next bastion of the "400," their seaside summer resort, Newport, Rhode Island. Alva would team up again with her mastermind builder, who would create a summer "cottage" seeming unconceivable. But Alva had big dreams from her earlier years in Paris, with the wallet to match, so the sky was the limit. Construction began in 1888 literally at the property right next to Mrs. Astor on tony Bellevue Avenue. It is unlikely the plot was chosen as a coincidence, most likely the positioning was done on purpose to show everyone who really was the Queen of society. The monster construction project was so involved and arduous, it took 4 years to complete. Special docks and warehouses were constructed along the waterfront to store all the materials needed to complete the complex project. More than 100 stone workers and craftsmen were brought to Newport from Italy, to work on the intricate details of the masterpiece under construction. They were sworn to secrecy and the entire building site was hidden behind high fences and tarps, Alva wanted the unveiling of her signature seaside palace to be a surprise, the likes of which, no one had ever seen, on U.S. shores anyway.

When the mansion was finally completed in 1892, Mr. William K. Vanderbilt officially gave the property to Alva, for the 39th birthday. When the property was finally unveiled, The Marble House went beyond even the harshest critics expectations. Mr. Hunt, the architect for the complex project, designed it after the Petit Trianon, a palace at Versailles, and literally spared no expense. The total cost was said to be 11 million dollars, with 7 million of the construction budget devoted to acquire 500,000 cubic feet of the desired and in some cases, rare stone. The Corinthian pilasters at the entrance were sourced from quarries in White Plains, New York. The 2-story entry hall features yellow Siena marble quarried from Italy and pink Numidian Marble adorns the walls of the dining room, all the way from North Africa. The gold covering the walls is 22 karat, and the bronze cast dining chairs were so heavy, a footman needed to be stationed behind each one to assist the guest when moving them.

It is unlikely such a place could even be completed today. It is improbable the craftsmen and artisans need to construct such an elaborate project could even be found to replicate the Marble House.

1895 would be a pivotal year for the aggressive social climber, with 2 major events occurring in the Vanderbilt's lives. Of course, Alva would cause controversy in both cases. Alva astonished New York society in March 1895 when she divorced her husband who had long been unfaithful, at a time when divorce was rare among the privileged, and received a large financial settlement said to be more than $10 million dollars. The grounds for divorce were allegations of William's philandering, although there were some rumors that Mr. Vanderbilt had hired a woman to pretend to appear to be a mistress so that Alva would finally divorce him. Perhaps he had just had enough of her socializing and focus on materialistic possessions.

The other monumental event was Alva's desire for a royal title for her family. Among the newly minted millionaires, there was a trend, to have a daughter, with a large dowry, to be married off to a European prince, count or duke. So, despite the fact Alva's daughter loved another man, she was literally forced to marry another man, against her wishes. Love be damned, Alva usually got what she wanted, and once again, wouldn't take no for an answer. She had locked Consuela in her room at the Marble House, threating to kill the man Consuela truly loved Winthrop Rutherfurd. Finally, Consuela relented, after Alva faked an illness, she claimed was caused by her daughter, and the stress over the marriage controversy. Consuelo Vanderbilt married Charles Spencer-Churchill, the 9th Duke of Marlborough at St. Thomas Episcopal Church, New York City, on November 6th, 1895. The pair would live in the drafty and cold Blenheim Palace in England and would have eventually have 2 children, mockingly called the "Heir and the Spare." The loveless, arranged marriage didn't last very long, when the couple finally separated in 1906, divorced in 1921, and the marriage was annulled, at the Duke's request.

The not so happy couple, The 9th Duke of Marlborough, Consuelo and their sons, John Spencer-Churchill, Marquess of Blandford, eventually the 10th Duke of Marlborough, and Lord Ivor Spencer-Churchill. Consuelo sarcastically referred to them as "the heir and the spare."

(This work is in the public domain in its country of origin.)

The year following her daughter's arranged, forced, and coerced nuptials, Alva would tie the knot again. She would marry her ex-husbands horseracing buddy, who lived down the street from the Marble House. Her earlier prediction had come to fruition, her 2nd marriage was for love. Although her new husband, Oliver Hazard Perry Belmont was no pauper, he was the heir to the Belmont banking fortune. His father, August Belmont, was the New York City representative of the powerful Rothschild banking house and included many of the business world's power brokers as his clients. If the Belmont name sounds vaguely familiar to you, it should. The 3rd leg of the prestigious horse racing triple crown, the Belmont Stakes, is named in the family's honor. OHP Belmont's Newport home was designed with his beloved horses in mind. Newport's favorite architect, Richard Morris Hunt, modeled Belcourt after a rural French hunting chateau, with a special twist. The first level of Belcourt was a stable, so after a long day of driving the horses and carriage around Ocean Drive, Mr. Belmont could open the gates and guide his beloved horses, directly through the side door and into their stalls. The beloved stallions even had silk sheets to keep them comfortable, with Mr. Belmont's personal living quarters were on the upper levels.

After marrying Alva, things would change drastically at Belcourt. The first-floor stable had to go and was redesigned into a grand ballroom to entertain her high society friends. So, as the new Mrs. Belmont moved in, the horses, they were moved out, relegated to the stable at the side of the property. Alva would also close up the Marble House to visitors, while she was living just down Bellevue Avenue at Belcourt. She would only store her clothes at Marble House because it had more ample closet space and to use the laundry, which was superior to the facilities at Belcourt. So essentially Alva had an 11 million storage unit with a laundry mat. Another demonstration of the excesses of the rich and famous during the Gilded Age!

After the sudden death of her 2nd husband, Oliver Belmont in 1908, Alva became extremely involved in the women's suffrage movement, in an effort to get women the right to vote. She even sent Richard Morris Hunt's sons to China, to draw up plans for an authentic Tea House, to be built on the Marble House grounds. This new addition would host many of Alva's suffrage events and is still part of the landscape today.

Ratified by Congress in August 1920, the 19th amendment finally gave women the right to vote and the woman who would not take no for an answer, triumphed once again.

Having seemingly accomplished everything she set out to do, Alva had moved to Paris, France to reconcile with her daughter Consuelo, who had married a French aviator. It seems Consuelo, like her mother, married for love the second go around as well. Since she no longer needed the Marble House, it was up for sale, and Mr. Frederick Prince of Boston, and the Armor Meatpacking Company, was the proud new owner. The sale price you ask, in 1932, at the height of the great depression? A mansion that cost 11 million dollars to construct, with 7 million spent on just the marble? $1, Mr. Prince paid one U.S. dollar, plus $99,000 for the interior furnishings. It was perhaps the greatest example of a real estate bubble in American History, at least up to that point and another example of why the Vanderbilts literally ran out of money.

Shortly after selling her Newport summer cottage, Alva had a debilitating stroke in 1932, and would pass away from a heart ailment, January 26th ,1933 at her Paris chateau. Her funeral was held back in New York City and true to form Alva did things a little bit differently than everyone else. Her funeral procession featured all female pallbearers with a large percentage of the mourners in attendance, her fellow, former suffragettes. Alva would be laid to rest next to Oliver Belmont, the husband she married for love, in the family mausoleum at Woodlawn Cemetery in the Bronx.

The final question would be for Alva, was it all worth it? Her New York City home, on 5th Avenue, Le Petit Chateau, was demolished in 1929, for a commercial building. That's where she spent $250,000 in one night, just to host a costume ball. Her Newport Mansion was eventually purchased from the Prince Family estate, by her youngest son, Harold Stirling Vanderbilt, and was donated to Newport's Preservation society, and is now open to the public as a museum. Was the forcing of her daughter to marry a man she didn't love worth the royal title, as Duchess of Marlborough? Perhaps her greatest claim to fame, was the passing of the 19th amendment, allowing women to vote. Somehow, all the social climbing and mansion building, in her one-track mind, was certainly worth it and it is unlikely, the stubborn, determined, and perseverant Alva

Erskine Smith Vanderbilt Belmont, wouldn't change a thing!

You are in luck, if you happen to be in Newport, Rhode Island, you can stop by and tour the Marble House. The property is a museum open to the public, and you yourself can see what 11 million dollars built in 1892 and what $1 bought 40 years later, in 1932.

www.newportmansions.org

The main character of the Gilded Age, Bertha Russell, is loosely based on Alva. Alva was tenacious and forced Old Money like Mrs. Astor to finally accept the deep pocketed Vanderbilts to high society. The story line in Gilded Age were Bertha Russell entices a prince with her daughter's hand in marriage along with her dowry, is completely based on a true story.

Alva Vanderbilt's ticket into high society included her 11 million dollars summer "Cottage," The Marble House. Built by architect Richard Morris Hunt and modeled after the Petit Trianon at Versailles.

(Photo courtesy of the author.)

17

Mrs. Make-A-Lister

Mrs. Caroline Astor has been called many things in her life in her role as the Queen of high society. After all, presiding over an ever-changing list of multi-generational family wealth, A – list Broadway performers, noteworthy politicians, and new class of super affluent titans of industry, was a fulltime job in itself. One she took deadly seriously. However, The Mrs. Astor, as she preferred to be called, felt it was her divine right as self-appointed "Queen" to determine which individuals and families were worthy enough to spend time in her presence. Quite an ego to say the least!

In her defense, Caroline (nee) Schermerhorn was born into New York City royalty so to speak, in 1830. She descended from the original Dutch aristocracy who founded the New Amsterdam colony, making their early fortunes from shipping, real estate, and the fur trade. Her extended family was considered one of the wealthiest and most influential with their shipping interests and vast real estate holdings, especially along the waterfront of Manhattan's lower east side. In 1853, her affluence would be taken to a whole new level, with her marriage to William Backhouse Astor, Jr. With his family's fur trapping, trading and real estate wealth and her impeccable pedigree, traceable to the original "Knickerbockers," Mrs. Astor was ready to create her rules, for society as she saw fit!

The first few decades of her marriage, Lina, as she was called in her younger days, focused her attention on raising her 5 children and construction of their new residence. New York City's new generation of wealth were moving up 5th Avenue and away from the more commercialized and crowded lower districts of Manhattan. In 1862, the Astors moved into their new 4 bay brownstone townhouse at 350 5th Avenue, next door to William's brother, John Jacob Astor III. Ironically, the area would eventually be redeveloped and is now where the iconic Empire State Building stands.

By the 1880's, with her children all grown up, Mrs. Astor turned her attention to what she viewed as her divine right. The ruler maker and dream taker of New York and eventually

Newport, high society. She alone possessed the power to include your family in polite society or shun them into oblivion and obscurity. In 1880, William Backhouse Astor purchased a seaside cottage in Newport, for a measly $190,000. Mrs. Astor then commissioned noted Architect Richard Morris Hunt, armed with a 2 million budget, to transform Beechwood into the epicenter of the City by the Sea's 8-week fashionable summer scene. The cottage, built in the 1850's, needed multiple upgrades to be able to host Mrs. Astor's exquisite tastes and her devoted disciples in style.

By the late 1880's Beechwood would be upgraded sufficiently to host Mrs. Astor's pride and joy, 'The 400." This was the exact number of people who she deemed to have the proper pedigree, a substantial amount of wealth generated over at least 3 generations and superior manners to be included in polite society. She would try to keep out the "nouveau riche" especially the railroad tycoons and their family's new money. The railroads were a dirty business in her opinion, but apparently overlooked the fact her husband's family wealth came from fur trapping. Mrs. Astor felt a fortune needed to age over many years, like a fine wine. She had help keeping her list as up to date as possible, with her social minister, Ward McAllister. He reasoned if you go outside that number, (400) "you strike people who are either not at ease in a ballroom or else make other people not at ease." Another, more plausible theory as to how they arrived at this number was, it was the capacity of Mrs. Astor's New York City ballroom. Either way, as you can imagine, this dynamic duo wielded an immense amount of power during the "Gilded Age."

McAllister called Mrs. Astor his mystic rose, and they would collaborate to plan some of Newport's most talked about and coveted dinner parties and galas, where admission was only permitted with a handwritten, hand delivered invitation from the Queen herself. The Vanderbilt's and their growing influence, power and massive wealth was becoming problematic for the mystic rose, despite the fact they were new money, the enormous amount of it they controlled was becoming too much to ignore. Another thorn in Mrs. Astors side was the pugnacious and perseverant social climber, Alva Vanderbilt, who would literally force her way into high society. Being married to William K. Vanderbilt, partial heir to the vast New York Central Railroad fortune certainly didn't hurt, when trying to break down the barrier to "The

400." But Alva was also cunning, she would turn the tables, and make the "Queen of High Society" beg her to be included.

In March of 1883, Alva would host a housewarming costume ball for 1200 illustrious guests, at her magnificent new 5th Avenue Mansion. As the story goes, Mrs. Astor's daughter, Carrie, was anxiously awaiting her invitation. After all, this was to be the highlight of this year's social calendar. Then the unthinkable happened, all her friends got their invitations but hers never arrived. Alva's trap had been set; she just needed the Astor's to walk into it! Due to the social norms and customs of that period, Alva claimed she could not invite Carrie Astor since Mrs. Astor had never officially called on the Vanderbilt home. Mrs. Astor really had no choice but to drop her visiting card at 660 5th Avenue, thus formally acknowledging the Vanderbilts. The Astors' invitation was received the next day, signaling the Vanderbilts reluctant inclusion into "The 400" at last.

By the late 1890's Mrs. Astor's grip on high society was waning and her 4-to-6-hour dinner parties were considered rather boring, by some of the new guard, who were now climbing the rungs of the social ladder themselves. Many of the stodgy old money families were dying off, or just not as interested in the prominence of the once powerful and coveted "400." Mrs. Astor's social minister, Mr.-Make-A -Lister himself, Ward McAllister passed away in 1895. At this time, a more lively, entertaining, and exciting party atmosphere was becoming the norm with Mrs. Astor's style of arduous multi course dinners and endless galas were a thing of the past.

Late in her life, she had moved in with her son, John Jacob Astor IV, further north on 5th avenue when she suffered a serious stroke, after falling down a flight of stairs. She was also suffering from dementia and withdrawn from the public eye. She would still wander her 5th Avenue Mansion in her finest evening wear, draped in her diamonds and calling out to party guests who had long since passed away. Perhaps she was reliving her glory days as the Queen of High Society in her mind, just one last time. Caroline Astor would pass away in October 1908 at the age of 78. Even in death, The Mrs. Astor would stand out above the rest, with a 39-foot-tall burial marker in the small Trinity Church Cemetery on the corner of Wall and Broad Streets in lower Manhattan. Her role as overseer of High Society was cumbersome, it took 3 women to take her place. Theresa Fair Oelrich of Rosecliff, Marion "Mamie" Fish of Crossway and the former thorn in her side, Alva Vanderbilt of The Marble House, commonly referred to as the "Triumvirate."

In 2010, a member of another list, purchased Mrs. Astors former summer home Beechwood, for 10.5 million dollars. Larry Ellison of the Oracle Corporation is a consistent member in the top 10 of the Forbes 400, a list of wealthiest Americans. Mr. Ellison has done extensive renovations to Beechwood, painstakingly refurbishing it to its 1881 glory, when The Mrs. Astor first burst upon the local social scene. His plan is to convert the first level into a public art museum, displaying his personal collection, with the second floor used for a private residence. Optimistically, she would be pleased with Mr. Ellisons preservation efforts, even though she would probably consider him, "New Money!"

The Queen of New York and Newport high society and the overseer of the "400," the Mrs. Astor. (This image is in the public domain in its country of origin.)

Mrs. Astor portrayal on the Gilded Age was accurate. She presided over high society with the assistance of her social minister, Ward McAllister. After her death, high society was managed by a trio of socialites. Mrs. Fish, Teresa Fair Olerich of Rosecliff and of course, Alva.

18

The Mansion on the Move

How does a massive structure like Seaview Terrace, begin its life in 1 city, then end up being rebuilt in another? Well, first and foremost, money, lots, and lots of money. Even Ripley's believe it or not, couldn't believe such a move could even take place...Yet it did, and we have the visual proof to show you. The interesting thing about the property is it covers all the bases as a Triple H kind of place, Historic, Hallowed, and Haunted!

Originally called Seaview Terrace is the 5th largest mansion in Newport RI. In 1907 millionaire Edson Bradley constructed a French-Gothic mansion in Washington D.C. It included a Gothic chapel with seating for 150 people, a large ballroom, an art gallery, and a 500-seat theater. When completed in 1911 it was called Aladdin's Palace.

In 1923 Mr. Bradley began disassembling Aladdin's Palace and started to relocate it to

Newport, Rhode Island. Not to worry, Mr. Bradley had deep pockets as the owner of a liquor distributorship and their very popular "Old Crow" whiskey.

Seaview Terrace was completed in 1925 as a compilation of new and old sections, incorporated into the Newport Estate Mr. Bradley had relocated from Washington D.C. In total Seaview Terrace cost over $2 million to construct.

Aladdin's Palace on Dupont Circle in Washington, DC. Before it's improbable relocation to Newport, RI.

(Photo courtesy of House Histree.)

In 1929 Mrs. Julia W. Bradley, wife of Edson Bradley, died and her funeral was held in the chapel inside the house. Mr. Bradley spent five summers at the mansion before his death in 1935. Julia B. Shipman, daughter of the Bradley, took possession of the estate and lived there until 1941. She vacated the house in 1942 after a dispute with the City of Newport over non-payment of three years of back taxes. During WWII the house was used by the US Army as an officer's quarters. In 1949 the property was purchased for $8,000.

From 1966 to 1971 the Gothic soap opera Dark Shadows used the mansion as the exterior shots for the fictional Collinwood Mansion. The show focused on a family of Vampires, living in Maine, headed by family patriarch Barnabus Collins. (In retrospect a family of vampires, living in Maine, doesn't seem all that farfetched!) Keep in mind, the series was not filmed on location in Newport. Most of the shows were shot primarily on location at the Lyndhurst estate in Tarrytown, New York. For the TV series, Essex, Connecticut was the locale used for the fictional town of Collinsport.

In 1974 Martin and Millicent Carey purchased the mansion. The Carey's faced a large cost for the upkeep and decided to lease the main house and gatehouse to Salve Regina University. The mansion was then renamed the Carey Mansion. In 2009 Salve Regina University terminated the lease with the Carey family which the university claimed was for lack of repairs and proper maintenance. But was there a more sinister reason?

Almost from the moment students moved into Carey Mansion, stories started about the mansion being haunted. It seemed that there was always something going on with the lights. Lights in rooms and hallways would constantly turn off and on without explanation. Students also remarked how their stereos would always turn on unexpectedly at all hours of the day and night. There was a rumor floating around campus that a nun had locked herself in an upstairs bedroom and wouldn't come out. Apparently, she thought she was possessed by Satan and would remain behind the locked door until the demon had left her body. But the demon would not leave her, so she took her own life. The university had the room sealed permanently and a priest would come by monthly to bless the demonically possessed area with holy water. However, this may have just been a rumor and has never been substantiated. But that doesn't mean the Carey Mansion isn't haunted. It is quite possibly the most haunted property on the entire campus. So, who is the mysterious ghost who roams the Carey Mansion? Julia Bradley, the wife of the original owner, also felt a great attachment to the place, so much so that many believe she has refused to move on in death.

She owned an Estey Organ, a fantastic piece of musical hardware, but unfortunately after she passed, and the house changed owners, the organ was allowed to enter a state of disrepair. The console was missing, making the organ no longer operational. This does not stop the ghost of Julia, who has been known to pipe up a tune or two on the organ - which cannot be played.

Even the popular TV show, Ghost Nation's crew members were mystified when they investigated the property. Almost immediately after entering the house, the ghost hunters heard some of the loudest overhead footsteps they had ever encountered. When the quickly checked the room above them it was completely empty. While investigating the organ room where Mrs. Bradley's ghost had been spotted on numerous occasions, they felt an impression on the bench where they were seated as if someone sat down to join them. They also felt an extreme drop in temperature, a sure sign that a ghostly presence was amongst them. They also encountered muffled voices behind walls and several doors that would abruptly open without any reasonable explanation. The Ghost Nation investigators themselves concluded; Carey Mansion was one of the most haunted places they had ever visited!

Seaview Terrace has recently hit the open market in 2021, for a whopping 29 million dollars. With more than 43,000 square feet of living space on 7+ acres, the property at 197 Ruggles Avenue has an abundance of space and an interesting backstory for a daring and deep pocketed buyer, as long as they don't mind sharing with a ghost or two!

Seaview Terrace casts a long, dark shadow over its neighbors on Ruggles Avenue. (Photo courtesy of the author.)

19

Cursed Fortune?

How could a family, with a fortune worth more than 200 million at one time, squander the entire amount, is less than 4 generations. Was it bad luck, a string of poor investments, not capitalizing on new, future industries, excessive partying, yacht, and mansion building and an uncontrollable gambling habit? Yes, yes, yes, and yes. Those factors certainly didn't help to preserve this clan's wealth estimated to be one of the top 5 all time, in the history of mankind and in less than 100 years, it was gone, POOF!

Or did this massive family fortune have a deeper, darker, and more sinister curse attached to it, almost seemingly damn all the men lined up to inherit the monster bankroll. Was it just a coincidence or was everyone in line to eventually receive the Vanderbilt Railroad fortune, doomed as soon as they were next in line, and ascend the proverbial throne?

Let's examine the details and the bizarre circumstances that each Vanderbilt male heir would suffer and make our decision.

Cornelius Vanderbilt started with humble beginnings in Staten Island, New York, in the early 1800's. He quit school at age 11 to work in his father's ferry business, between Staten Island and lower Manhattan. At 16, the young entrepreneur launched his own ferry service, thanks to a $100 loan from his mother. Cornelius purchased a periauger, a narrow draft twins masted sailboat, and carried passengers and freight across New York Bay. Other, more seasoned boat captains were amazed by the enthusiasm of this young sailor and started calling him "The Commodore" and it would stick, for the rest of his life.

By the 1840's, the Commodore was well established as steamship operator along the Hudson River, along the east coast of the United States, and even ferrying passengers to Central America for prospectors to traverse the isthmus on their way to the California gold fields. He had a large, growing family of 13 children, with his wife, and cousin by the way, Sophia Johnson. Business was good for the Commodore, but he wasn't satisfied, setting his sights on a new transportation method. This new mode of travel would revolutionize commuting and commerce while making him one of the wealthiest men of all time. The Commodore saw the future and railroads would revolutionize travel and commerce, especially around America's largest city and metro area. He started purchasing many of the smaller regional lines around Manhattan, eventually consolidating them into a massive corporation, The New York Central Railroad. The New York Central would control freight and passenger service throughout the metro area and was the only rail service in and out of Manhattan for almost a century. Certainly, with 4 sons of his 13 children, Cornelius Vanderbilt would find a capable male heir to one day take over his railroad empire.

Commodore Cornelius Vanderbilt, founder of the family fortune.

(Image acquired in the public domain.)

The Commodore's last-born son, George Washington Vanderbilt, was his pride and joy. Cornelius and Sophia had named an earlier child George, but sadly, the toddler died at age 4. This George was big and strong like his father, he reportedly could deadlift over 900 pounds and was trained as an army officer at prestigious West Point. Surely, he would be the successor to his father's railroad empire, ushering it into the century and beyond. Tragically, the young army officer would be critically injured at the Battle of Shiloh, eventually dying from his wounds and a bout of Tuberculosis in 1864. The next in line would be Cornelius Jerimiah, but things did not look promising for the young Vanderbilt. He frequently suffered from epileptic seizures and was considered meek and a bit of a mama's boy by the hard driving Commodore. In 1849, Corneel, was sent on a ship headed for San Francisco around Cape Horn to work as a crew member. His father thought the long journey would "toughen up" his lackadaisical son. When Corneel finally arrived in San Francisco, he abandoned the ship and spent all his money on liquor and gambling. When he ran out, of cash he tried to charge his expenses to his father, who became livid and was convinced Corneel's actions were a sign of insanity. When Corneel returned to New York in November 1849, his father had him arrested and committed to the Bloomingdale Insane Asylum in New York until February 1850. Corneel would move to East

Hartford, Connecticut to attempt to elude the reach of his influential dad. Corneel ran an unsuccessful fruit farm and had to rely on a small family allowance and loans from family friends to make ends meet. His last hope was an inheritance from his father's estate, but his hopes were dashed, when it was revealed 95% of the fortune would go to his brother, Billy. Soon after hearing the devastating news, Corneel would go on one last gambling and drinking spree, before taking his life at the Glenham Hotel on 5th Avenue in 1882.

By process of elimination, there was only one male heir remaining, who could run the family business, eldest son Billy. Cornelius frequently berated and criticized him, calling his first-born son a "blockhead" and a "blatherskite". Billy worked feverishly to show his father that he was not, in fact, a blatherskite, and proved his business acumen by turning around the Staten Island Railway and making a profit. Apparently, he had done enough to earn his father's trust, because after the Commodore's passing in 1877, William Henry Vanderbilt was named principal heir. The Commodore, in naming a successor, did what the nobility in Europe was famous for, leaving the bulk of their wealth and property to one primary heir. This would be the case with the New York Central Railroad estate, William Henry, i.e., Billy, got the bulk of the cash, 100 million dollars!

William Henry was a capable successor, expanding the railroad profits and increasing his personal wealth to over 200 million dollars, an astronomical amount, by 1885. Perhaps the stress of managing a multi-million-dollar enterprise was overwhelming or the curse of the fortune was a real thing. Either way, William Henry died unexpectedly in December 1885 at the relatively young age of 64. The misfortune of wielding the hefty burden, was about to be passed to the next generation of Vanderbilt heirs…

The bulk of the Vanderbilt's extensive wealth came from their ownership of the New York Central Railroad.

(Image acquired in the public domain.)

Cornelius Vanderbilt II would ascend to the proverbial throne and take over as chairman of the volatile and stressful Railroad business. This is also where the connection to Newport, Rhode Island would begin, as this 3rd generation of young tycoons, would go about spending the large cash piles the first 2 generations had built. Cornelius II would purchase a seaside wooden cottage overlooking the Atlantic Ocean in 1885, from fellow business magnate Pierre Lorillard IV, called The Breakers. The cozy seaside cottage would burn to the ground in November 1892, so the deep pocketed Vanderbilt, quickly summoned the family's favorite architect, Richard Morris Hunt, to create a signature summer home that would show the world, who was the richest of them all.

Mr. Hunt did not disappoint, with his majestic 2nd version of the Breakers, completed at a breakneck speed, opening in 1895, just 2 years after the earlier fire. This mansion was built to be fireproof, with the furnace located at the entrance to the grounds, hidden under the gatehouse. A massive tunnel, large enough to drive a team of horses through, would deliver heat into the Breakers. And why would a summer home need a furnace, you might ask? It was mostly used during the winter months to preserve the artwork and tapestries as well as keep the caretaker and his family warm. They would occupy the drafty space throughout the winter, after the owners packed up and returned to NYC for the winter. The massive kitchen would also be offset from the main part of the Mansion so in case of a fire, the cooking space could be sealed off from the rest of the rooms and prevent the blaze from spreading.

The Italian Renaissance "cottage" was inspired by 16th century merchant palaces in Genoa and Turin, and features 70 rooms, with over 100,000 square feet, spread out over 5 levels. The impressive 2 story entry way, known as the Great Hall, is designed to look like an Italian Courtyard, with the ceiling painted to resemble a blue, cloud swept sky. The Breaker's footprint is so vast, it takes up an entire acre of the 14-seaside acre plot overlooking Cliffwalk and the Atlantic Ocean. Why would Mrs. Alice Vanderbilt refer the Breakers as her cottage? Because her New York City mansion at 1 West 57th Street was double the size, with a colossal 140 rooms, covering an entire Manhattan city block.

Mr. Vanderbilt did not get to enjoy his new seaside palace very long, however. The chairman suffered a debilitating stroke in 1896, confining him to a wheelchair, and severely curtailing his involvement in the day-to -day operations of the railroad. Unexpectedly, he would suffer a final, fatal cerebral hemorrhage in 1899, at the tragically young age of 55. Once again, the unwieldy responsibility of overseeing the New York Central, claimed another victim. The responsibility of being named 'The Richest Man" in America, carried a heavy price.

As the railroad prosperity was conveyed to the 4th Vanderbilt generation, the previous results did not bode well for those next in line for the crown. Cornelius II and Alice's oldest son was William Henry Vanderbilt, a studious lad by all accounts, who studied at Yale University, and likely his father's choice to step in one day as chairman of the New York Central. Unfortunately, he would never be given the opportunity after contracting Typhoid fever and passing away at the tender age of 21.

Next up would be Cornelius Vanderbilt III, who was commonly known as "Neily" perhaps in an effort to avoid confusion with all the other Cornelius Vanderbilts. To many observers, Neily would have been an outstanding choice as successor to run the Railroad operation. He had graduated from Yale, with a degree in mechanical engineering and had a true interest in the railroad business, always tinkering with trains in his spare time. He would eventually have 30 patents on his resume for improvements to locomotives and rail cars. Neily would never get the chance to run his family business however, after marrying a woman named Grace Wilson. His parents did not approve of the older woman, and her reportedly promiscuous past, as well as her father's deceptive business practices during the Civil War. Many business insiders considered Grace Wilson's father a war profiteer. After literally coming to blows with his father, Cornelius II, Neily was written out of the will, and the wealth would be passed to the next in line. This decision would cost Neily roughly 50 million dollars in lost inheritance and he wouldn't talk to his mother Alice again, for 27 years. Coincidentally, 3 days after the physical altercation with Neily, the family patriarch would suffer his debilitating stroke from which he would never completely recover.

If you can envision the incarnation of a 1900's dapper, suave and debonair multi-millionaire beneficiary of a business tycoon's fortune, he would resemble Alfred Gwynne Vanderbilt. "Freddy" was also a Yale graduate, class of 1899, where he was a member of the exclusive, yet secretive "skull and bones" society. After graduation, Vanderbilt and a group of close friends set off on a two year around the world journey. Upon reaching Japan in September, young Alfred received word that his father had died, and quickly cut the trip short, and headed back to New York City. Upon his arrival, Alfred was informed he was the principal heir to his father's sizable fortune, roughly 36 million dollars, as well as his father's horse farm in Portsmouth, Rhode Island. The new head of the Vanderbilt family had little interest in the day-to-day intricacies of the railroad, and his large bankroll allowed Alfred to pursue 3 of his favorite passions, Horse Racing, Travel and Womanizing. In April of 1912, Alfred had booked passage on the new luxury Liner, the Titanic, sailing from Southampton, England. Fate would intervein and the very fortunate Alfred, extended his London holiday, avoiding almost certain death in the icy North Atlantic. Alfred's luck would run out 3 years later, when he sailed to Liverpool, England to attend the International Horse Breeders Association on the R.M.S. Lusitania. There were warnings posted in New York City newspapers the day before departure, the R.M.S. Lusitania was sailing through a warzone, and if carrying war munitions, could be targeted by the German Navy. There was even a rumor that someone slipped a note under Alfred's hotel room door, telling him the Lusitania would be targeted...Yet despite the warnings, Alfred sailed anyway, accompanied by his valet and a mistress. Less than 8 miles off the head of Old Kinsale, Ireland, the Lusitania was struck by a torpedo, launched from a Germany submarine, the U20. 1198 passengers perished when the luxury liner sank in a remarkable 18 minutes including Alfred Gwynne Vanderbilt. A witness said, Alfred gave a young mother and her daughter his lifebelt, when hers could not be in the panic ensuing on deck. This was certainly a heroic action on Mr. Vanderbilt's part, since the globetrotting, multi-millionaire playboy, never learned to swim. And despite a $1000 reward for Alfred's body, it was never recovered, and another Vanderbilt head of the family was gone at age 37.

Alfred Gwynne Vanderbilt, the dashing young heir to the Vanderbilt fortune, perished when the Lusitania sank in only 18 minutes.

(Image acquired in the public domain.)

There was one last hope for a successor to take charge of the family business, Reginald Claypool Vanderbilt, the youngest son of Cornelius II and Alice. If you looked up in the dictionary the definition of spoiled, entitled, inebriated, compulsive gambling, trust fund frat boy, it's likely Reggie's picture would accompany the description. Reginald also had very little interest in managing the New York Central. He was exceptional at spending money on breeding horses, running over pedestrians in his fancy motor cars and drinking way too many brandy milk punches at the exclusive men's only club, the Newport Reading Room. Reginald had purchased a large property, called Sandy Point Farm in Portsmouth, Rhode Island, where he raised thoroughbreds and polo ponies. He was also notorious for loosing hundreds of thousands of dollars in Richard Canfield's clandestine gambling halls in New York and Newport. In 1923, Reginald aged 42, married a 17-year-old named Gloria Morgan and together they had a child, little Gloria. Reginald, who had been diagnosed with cirrhosis of the liver at the age of 23, was experiencing serious nosebleeds and stomach pains. A doctor confirmed the fears, his liver was severely damaged from years of heavy drinking. The dire warning from the physician was to swear off booze, or Reginald would be dead, period, end of story!

Gloria had traveled to Chile to attend to her ailing mother, leaving Reginald to his own devices, which in hindsight, probably wasn't a great idea. When Gloria arrived at Sandy Point Farm, she noticed her mother in law's Rolls Royce in the driveway, and immediately knew something was terribly wrong. After another night of heavy drinking, at some of Newport's famous watering holes, Reginald Claypoole Vanderbilt was found dead of alcohol poisoning liver failure at age 45.

Gloria Morgan, Little Gloria, and Reginald Claypoole Vanderbilt, shortly before his death from alcohol poisoning and cirrhosis of the liver. Little Gloria is the mother of CNN on air personality Anerson Cooper.

(Image acquired in the public domain.)

So, was the Vanderbilt fortune cursed? The misfortune was probably due the burden of managing such a massive and cumbersome corporation, which at one time was the largest employer in the country. The stress, poor diets, excessive drinking and access to luxuries not available to the common man, likely placed undue anxiety and pressure on the Vanderbilt heirs, cutting their lives short. It is rather alarming that a family, with at one point in their history, controlled over 200 million dollars, and could squander it all. The mansions and summer cottages that still exist are mostly museums, including the Marble House, and Rhode Island's most visited tourist attraction, The Breakers. They stand as a reminder of an era of unprecedented growth, commerce, and prosperity nearly unparalleled in world history. The vast and almost unfathomable fortunes created from new industries and technologies like railroads, steel production, oil refining, automobile manufacturing, Real Estate speculation, Investment Banking and mining serve as a tribute to an era of excesses. The trust funds were funded with New York Central Railroad stock, once the bedrock of Wall Street, with an elevated price and a healthy dividend. By the end of World War II, rail travel was in decline, especially with the rise of Air Travel and the Automobile, and the one time darling of Wall Street was bankrupt. The rail line merged with a few other competitors and evolved into Conrail, by the 1970's.

Little Gloria was the best-known Vanderbilt of the 20th century, with her Jeans enterprise. I can honestly say, my first memory of hearing the name Vanderbilt, was the Jeans commercials in the 1980's. If you are of a certain age, you probably remember the ads featuring singer Blondie, a young Gina Davis, "George Jefferson" Sherman Hemsley and of course Gloria herself promoting her new stretch denim jeans. On June 17,2019 one of the last links to the Vanderbilt's past glory, passed away at age 95. The sad news was announced to the world by her son, who now carries on the family legacy, CNN on air personality, Anderson Cooper. She is buried next to her son Carter and late her husband Wyatt adjacent to the Vanderbilt mausoleum in the Moravian Cemetery on Staten Island, New York. May they all rest in peace!

The prophetic words of Commodore Vanderbilt were certainly apropos, especially when it came to the financial fate of his own family: "Any fool can make a million dollars, but it takes a man of brains to keep it after he has made it." Well said, Commodore, well said.

The Breakers Mansion, the crown jewel of the Newport, RI. summer "Cottages" along Bellevue Avenue and the Cliff walk.

(Photo courtesy of the author.)

Fans of the Gilded Age will recognize the Breakers from Season 1. Episode 9, where the music room was used for the setting of Gladys Russell's debutant ball.

20

The most robbed Woman in America

"Bois Dore", literally translated from French, means golden wood or gilded forest, so pardon my French. For some of the owners of this gilded mansion, things were far from Golden…

Completed in 1927, the Classic French Chateau style mansion was built for William Fahnestock, an investment banker whose extended family were founding members of one of Citigroup's many predecessors, the First National Bank of New York. Mr. Fahnestock was an unabashed Francophile, which means he loved all things French. Even the trees lining the driveway were imported from his beloved France, to add a European touch. The noble and majestic Linden Trees that shade the drive, would be decorated with 18 karat golden apples as a special welcome to guests and accessorize the "Gilded Forest."

The entrance to the "Gilded Forest" with the imported Linden Trees.

(Image courtesy of Wikimedia.)

The property, which has long been considered one of the last Grand Estates built toward the end of the Gilded Age, was eventually purchased by a Campell Soup heiress, Elinor Winifred Dorrance Hill Ingersoll and her husband, Vice Admiral Stuart Ingersoll. You see, Elinor was the granddaughter of a chemist named John Dorrance, who worked at Campbell soup. He patented the process to make condensed soup in a can, eventually making enough money as owner of the patent, he bought the soup company from the Campbell family. Now more than 100 years later, that patent is still paying dividends for his heirs and descendants.

Carolyn Mary Skelly purchased the mansion in 1978 and hung a portrait of her father on the grand staircase. Her daddy was in the Oklahoma and Texas oil business, eventually merging his company with Getty Oil. After her husband's passing, she partied well into her 80's, being frequently seen on the dance floors of many Newport Clubs, where DJs would play "Sweet Caroline" for her. Carolyn had a fabulous collection of jewelry which over the years has made her a seemingly easy target for criminals, including an armed robbery at Bois Dore'. In August of 1986, a masked, knife wielding intruder, entered the 2nd floor and ordered Carloyn by name, to direct him to her jewelry collection. ''I feel so lost without them,' Skelly would later say of her stolen jewelry, which included a 50-carat diamond ring and a large square sapphire ring surrounded by diamonds.

''I was just petrified. I couldn't utter a sound; Skelly would recall as she described her encounter with the ski masked robber inside the second-floor bedroom of her 36-room mansion. The estimates of the total value of jewelry taken from Bois Dore' was 5 million dollars. Amazingly and probably not coincidently, this was the 5th time Carolyn Skelly had pieces of her extensive jewelry collection stolen.

In 1977, she was robbed of $199,000 in uninsured jewels at her Southampton, N.Y., mansion. In 1982, Skelly was robbed of $1 million in uninsured jewelry outside LaGuardia Airport. In August 1984, Skelly was also robbed of $2.2 million in gold and jewelry by a former maid at her Newport mansion. In August 1985, three teenagers broke into her estate and stole about 15 pieces of gold and diamond jewelry, the value of which was not estimated. In the last 2 cases the stolen items were recovered.

It is estimated Carolyn Skelly had more than 20 million dollars of jewelry heisted over the years and was dubbed "The most robbed woman in America" by the Boston Globe, certainly not a title anyone aspires to receive. After the 5th incident, Carolyn remarked, she has finally learned her lesson. She would hire a full-time security guard, turn on her electronic surveillance and burglar alarms and most importantly, only buy and wear costume jewelry, going forward.

21

In Your Face
(Mrs. Astor)

Edward Berwind didn't really care much about the pomp and circumstance involving the inner squabbling of New York and Newport high society and Mrs. Astor's exclusive "400." He was a very busy businessman, running his enterprise, The Berwind White Coal Company.

Mr. Berwind was a graduate of the Naval Academy, with his nomination coming from none other than President Abraham Lincoln. During the Grant administration, Berwind served as a Naval Attache at the White House. Mr. Berwind was able to leverage his military connections to secure large contracts to supply the U.S. Navy with coal, their main source of power around the turn of the last century. Berwind coal would also power steamships and railroads, the backbone of early 20th century commerce. As the owner of the largest coal fields and mines in Western Pennsylvania, Kentucky and West Virginia, the seemingly endless appetite for the carbon-based fuel source made Mr. Berwind a very wealthy man.

After summering at a modest beach cottage, for many years, Mr. Berwind, and his wife Sarah, embarked on building their own signature "Cottage" along Millionaire's Row, Bellevue Avenue. Philadelphia architect, Horace Trumbauer was commissioned to create the Berwind's summer wonderland, after creating numerous other exquisite French inspired chateaus along the high-end thoroughfare. The result was the Elms, completed in 1901, and inspired by the Château d'Asnières, an 18th century dwelling in a suburb of Paris, France. Mr. Berwind was keenly interested in technology, and The Elms was one of the first houses in America to be wired for electricity. The house also included one of the first electrical ice makers, which came in handy for large summer parties. There is also a hidden coal chute, on the adjacent Dixon Street, with a small underground rail line, to shuttle the coal into the basement furnace generator which illuminated the home. This way the delivery of the coal was shielded from the Mansion's occupants and guests.

The Elms also features an expansive sunken garden, roughly 11 acres, shaded by large Elm and Weeping Beech Trees, painstaking cultivated by noted landscape architect E. W. Bowditch.

The Elms features a beautifully flowered and landscaped sunken garden. (Image courtesy of New England Gardens and Assoc.)

Mr. Berwind and his wife both enjoyed entertaining their own close-knit circle of friends and business contacts. Mrs. Astor, the self-appointed overseer of New York and Newport's old money high society. She went out of her way to ostracize, what she considered "the new money" which included the Railroad Tycoons and the Coal Barons. Mrs. Astor considered coal a dirty business and vowed never to include anyone who profited from it to be included in her cadre, "The 400." Mr. Berwind was certainly aware of the burgeoning cold war brewing along Bellevue Avenue, between the two groups. As a not-so-subtle way to tweak the socially conscious Caroline Astor, Mr. Berwind fired a loud warning shot across her bow, announcing he was here to stay. On the flower urns atop the front wall at the Elms, Mr. Berwind prominently displayed his portrait more than a dozen times, on both sides of the ceramic vases. This way Mrs. Astor was forced to see his face as she was both coming and going to her Newport summer cottage, Beechwood. This was Mr. Berwind's passive aggressive way to say "In your face, Mrs. Astor" I don't need you and your high society. I have my own influential circle of friends and business associates, including Secretary of the Navy, and future President, Theodore

Roosevelt, King Wilhelm II of Germany and Edward VII, King of England.

After Mr. Berwind's passing in 1936, his sister Julia would continue entertaining at the Elms until 1961. That's when the controversy over the Elms future began. A nephew who inherited the estate, had no interest in retaining the property, and sold it to a developer. The developer had planned to tear down the Chateau and redevelop the gardens, into a Howard Johnsons Motor Lodge. Can you imagine? Thankfully, the Preservation Society quickly raised sufficient funds, just over $100,000 dollars, and saved the irreplaceable mansion from the wrecking ball and now operate the property as a museum.

If you ever have the privilege of visiting Newport, Rhode Island and are intrigued by the inner workings of a Gilded Era mansion, take the guided "Servants Life Tour" tour of the Elms. The tour moves you from the basement kitchens, coal cellar and boiler room, laundry rooms and wine cellar, to the third-floor staff quarters, where you'll see a large water collecting cistern and a roof top deck with great views of the property.

Don't forget to say hi to Mr. Berwind, or at least his caricature on the flower urns, still defiantly gazing down upon passersby along Bellevue Avenue, no doubt with an eye out for Mrs. Astor.

Mr. Berwind's caricature is forever "in your face" and perpetually keeping a watchful eye on passersby along Bellevue Avenue.

(Photo courtesy of the author.)

The Elms will be familiar to fans of the Gilded Age on HBO. It was Mrs. Russell's Newport summer home where Bertha and Ward McAllister are seen walking across the law. The Elms kitchen is also featured prominently depicting the Russell's New York City Mansion, with multiple scenes featuring Mr. Church, Mr. Watson, Mrs. Bruce and Chef Boudin.

22

Get down off your High Horse

If you are a fan of the game of Tennis, and who isn't, you can thank a dare from August 1879 for the Tennis Hall of Fame's location in Newport, Rhode Island. If you are a bit confused, don't worry, it will all make sense shortly. There is also a polo pony, a stodgy private men's club and impulsive newspaper publisher involved as well.

The saga began at the Newport Reading Room, which was founded in 1854, and is an exclusive men's only private club, for the movers and shakers of the seaside summer colony. Picture if you will, septuagenarians with top hats, monocles, and ascots, seated in leather high back chairs, sipping cognac out of a snifter, and smoking Cuban cigars in front of a fireplace. The conversation at the Reading Rooms probably dealt with the manipulation of railroad stocks, lamenting the high wages the unions were demanding and trying to corner to the gold market. Much like Randolph and Mortimer Duke, trying unsuccessfully to corner the Frozen Concentrated Orange Juice Market in Trading Places. (1980's pop culture reference.) I would surmise these gentlemen of leisure would say "Yes" "Quite" and "Indeed" rather frequently between brandy sips and cigar puffs.

The New York Herald Publisher was no stranger to controversy. James Gordon Bennet Jr. had become a wealthy man from his outlandish headlines, and newspaper sagas, including funding the journey of Henry Stanley, finally locating Dr. Livingston in Africa. The narrative ended with the headline published in the Herald in 1869, *"Dr Livingston I Presume?"* He had also been engaged to marry New York socialite Caroline May in 1877. However, the hard drinking publisher arrived late to a dinner to meet her parents, extremely intoxicated, and from all accounts, urinated in the fireplace in full view of the astonished and appalled guests. As you can imagine, the wedding was called off and Bennet laid low in Paris for a while, when an account of the debacle ended up being published in the Guiness Book of World Records as the most embarrassing engagement dinner in history!

On an early August afternoon in 1879, New York Herald Newspaper magnate James Gordon Bennet Jr. and his polo playing partner Henry Augustus "Sugar" Candy were having drinks at the Reading Room. Bennet and Candy were instrumental in bringing polo to the U.S. with the founding of the Westchester Polo Club. "Sugar" Candy was a proficient polo player, horseman, and Captain of the British Team. By all accounts the pair of troublemakers were quite inebriated and seemingly bored. As the story goes, Bennett dared his mate to ride his horse onto the front porch of the Reading Room, to liven things up a bit. "Sugar" Candy took the dare one step further and rode straight through the clubrooms, disturbing the shocked and outraged members.

The startled members, probably awoken from their afternoon naps, implored Candy to stop the commotion, shouting:

"Get down off your high horse Candy!"
(Illustration by Bailey.)

Even the staff tried to warn him about his antics when a white jacketed butler, remarked, politely yet forcefully, "Sir, you cannot ride your horse in here!" Candy ignored the appeal and continued on his equestrian jaunt through the Club.

Candy's guest membership was revoked, and Bennett was censured by the infuriated and incensed members. The impetuous and impulsive publisher purchased the land across the street from his home, Stone Villa, and vowed to build his own social club. He was done with the stuffy and uninteresting Reading Room.

Bennett hired the preeminent design firm, of its day, McKim, Mead and White to design his new state of the art social club. Stanford White, the flashy and flamboyant architect, would lead the project. Completed in 6 short months, the new club opened on August 2nd, 1880, with more than 3,000 visitors passing through the ample stone archway. The Newport Casino offered a block of shops on Bellevue Avenue, a restaurant and gentlemen's lodging. Activities included archery, billiards, concerts, dancing, dining, horse shows, lawn bowling, with a separate theater building for plays. There were also grass courts for the newly introduced sport, lawn tennis, croquet, and court tennis. The Newport Daily News bragged, "It is doubtful if a livelier place can be found." The Casino, which means "Little House" in Italian, (not a gambling hall) also permitted day memberships for anyone to come in and enjoy the facilities. Something the Reading Room would never consider.

The stately shingle style structure was also home to the first lawn tennis championships, the forerunner to the U.S. Tennis open. The championships were held on the grass courts from 1881 to 1915, before the open was relocated to a larger facility in Forest Hills, New York. The boastful, brash, and boisterous James Gordon Bennett hit it out of the park, with creation of the Newport Casino.

By the 1950's the club's business had decreased substantially, and the main building was in disrepair. Jimmy Van Alen, a local sportsman, tennis aficionado and the inventor of the tie breaker scoring system, had a solution to the Casino's slumping revenue. He teamed with the U.S. tennis association to establish the International Tennis Hall of Fame inside the historic Casino Complex. It was a match made in heaven. Since 1955 there have been more than 260 inductees including players, coaches, announcers, and contributors from the world of Tennis, hailing from over 27 countries, making it truly International. The grass courts also host the only Men's professional tournament in

North America contested on the manicured lawns, making it a well-attended sporting event in July, boosting Newport's tourism.

And if you are ever on Jeopardy and the Answer is: Which seaside resort city hosted both the first U.S. Tennis and Golf Opens? What is Newport, Rhode Island?

The Gilded Age used the Casino for multiple episodes especially for the tennis events and Mr. McAllister's annual summer soirée.

The Fashionable Newport Casino was built as the result of dare. It is now home to the International Tennis Hall of Fame.

(Image courtesy of the author.)

23

Darkness on the edge of Town

Newport, Rhode Island has certainly had its fair share of eccentrics and generally bizarre characters over its 380 + years of existence. There is one resident, however, who stands head and shoulders above them all. Her name was Beatrice Turner. Beatrice was born in 1888 to a wealthy Philadelphia cotton broker named Andrew Turner and his wife Adele. As much as Mr. Turner was a successful businessman, he also had a spiritual, eclectic side as well. He would frequently pen odd and incomprehensible poems and would spend hours trying to interpret the true meaning of his dreams. He was also overly defensive of his only child, sometimes to a fault. From a young age, Beatrice showed a propensity for painting and was accepted to the prestigious Pennsylvania Academy of Fine Arts. However, her overbearing father pulled her out of school when he discovered painting nudes was part of the academy's curriculum. Andrew's advice to the budding artist was to focus her talents to painting family members and especially self-portraits. She would take his advice to heart, becoming the first selfie queen of the 20th century.

In 1907 the Turner's purchased the estate of a former Maryland Governor, perched on a hill overlooking the Cliff walk, and named their new summer home, Arcadia. Even in Newport, Beatrice could not escape the watchful eye of her overbearing father, including being chastised for walking with a boy on the seaside pathway. It appeared Andrew was trying to keep young Beatrice sequestered and away from anyone but him. Rumor began to fly that Beatrice was being inappropriately touched by her dad and her future behavior points to that possibility.

In 1913, Andrew returned to Philadelphia to open the family brownstone for the upcoming season and was found dead with obvious cause, the next day. Beatrice was devastated with the sudden and unexpected passing of her cherished father and to say she would never be the same again, would be a massive understatement. Andrew had left one last poem for his introverted daughter to interpret:

> " I dreamed I dwelt in a house of black.
>
> Located in the land of Arcadia.
>
> And absolutely nothing did it lack.
>
> For I was with my two sweethearts."
>
> "I awoke and found I was in a house of Brown.
>
> Far from loving glances and melodious voices.
>
> O when we are so far from those we love.
>
> Don't such dreams last until we meet again?"

Of course, the poem is open to interpretation and young Beatrice took his final message quite literally. She did the unthinkable and inexplicable, she immediately had the entire seaside property painted funeral black, just as she thought her late father had cryptically instructed. It remained this dark and ominous color until the day she died. Beatrice also wouldn't allow her father's body to be buried, propping his lifeless corpse up in bed, until she could complete one final portrait. As a lasting tribute to her spiritualist father, she would be dressed in black, Victorian clothing for the remainder of her days. Her stunned neighbors reported she would even wear the grim, grieving garments even when performing common household tasks, like mowing the lawn and raking leaves. Ms. Turner would never marry but was seen frequently walking as a dark solitary figure, alone, along the Cliff walk, below her darkened home.

When Beatrice passed away in 1948, it was revealed, finally, what the mysterious recluse did in her free time. Ms. Turner passed with no heirs and the house would be sold and the contents would be discarded. Once the new owners stepped inside the seaside manor, it was revealed what the reclusive Beatrice Turner did with her free time. She painted a lot! 3000 pieces of art were discovered throughout the vast home with more than 1000 self-portraits of the artist herself! However, the new owners were not impressed and most of the paintings were hauled off to the town landfill. What wasn't hauled away was set ablaze in a massive bonfire on the back lawn of the mansion. Some alert and conscientious neighbors were able to salvage some of the precious paintings, but most of her lifetime of artwork, literally went up in smoke.

New ownership purchased the property in the late 1980's and embarked on a painstaking refurbishment, to restore the seaside manor, to its original 19th century glory, without the funeral black exterior of course. The latest owners would even track down some of Beatrice's handywork, and proudly display the rare portraits inside their new creation, a luxury bed and breakfast, The Cliffside Inn.

Beatrice Turner's complex and complicated legacy will always be a part of Newport lore. She will forever be remembered as a talented, yet reclusive artist whose flower was never allowed to bloom because of her overbearing and possibly abusive father. Her surviving paintings are a sad reminder of what might have become of Beatrice Turner had she been allowed to pursue her true passion.

But Beatrice may not have left us after all! Her spirit is a frequent visitor to the Cliffside Inn. Numerous guests have reported a full body apparition standing at the foot of their bed in what was once Beatrice's bedroom. Front desk employees have witnessed a figure dressed in black descend the long staircase and passing effortlessly through the closed front door. The shadowy figure would pass literally through the solid door, never breaking stride on her way to the seaside trail. Beatrice's ghost has also been seen numerous times wandering the Cliff walk at various locations along the 3-and-a-half-mile path. Typically, the dark, solemn figure is seen head down and moving at a brisk pace, with the phantom, never picking up its head or making eye contact. Witness' have tried to catch up to the spectral figure but usually the ghost always remains just out of reach, never allowing anyone to catch up to get a closer look. There is one sure way to identify the ghost of Beatrice Turner. Look for a solitary figure walking along the Cliff walk, moving fast, never looking up and always fully dressed in black! Beatrice was a recluse in life and that continues, even in death: her spirit remains elusive, reclusive, and mysterious...

The beautiful Cliffside Inn was once painted all black by the enigmatic and eccentric Beatrice Turner.

(Photo courtesy of the author.)

Made in the USA
Columbia, SC
26 September 2025